Understanding Our World Through Geography

by
Jerry Aten

illustrated by Marilynn Barr

Cover by Jeff Van Kanegan

Copyright © Good Apple, 1991

ISBN No. 0-86653-592-6

Printing No. 987654

Good Apple
A Division of Frank Schaffer Publications, Inc.
23740 Hawthorne Boulevard
Torrance, CA 90505-5927

TABLE OF CONTENTS

GA1309

GA1309

MESSAGE TO THE TEACHER

Year after year of national testing continues to show less than satisfying results of student knowledge and understanding of basic geography skills. The results might well be even more dismal if the adult population were tested. Because the United States is a powerful nation offering continued assistance to others all over the world, we have become internationalists. Yet we are very weak when it comes to knowing even our own country.

With our planet in peril, there is an almost obligatory wave of support for placing more emphasis on a knowledge of our earth. At the very base of that knowledge must lie an adequate grasp of geography skills and concepts. That is, in reality, what this book is all about. You will find an obvious "save-the-planet" and "you-can-make-a-difference" theme woven into many of the activities and projects. Yet the main focus remains on improving geography skills and knowledge of basic concepts.

The book is divided into several sections that combine to make it a convenient resource for the teacher. The first part includes activities that will enrich and reinforce a number of map reading skills. Becoming familiar with the use of a compass, learning directions, examining different kinds of maps, learning about latitude and longitude, time zones and developing proficiency in reading various kinds of maps are the objectives of this first section of the book.

The next section examines a number of concepts and definitions that are most important in developing an understanding of geography. Each term begins with a brief explanation, followed by activities that get students involved in further investigation. Some of the activities are research-based; others employ the discovery method; still others require map reading skills. Many of the activities were designed to improve student writing potential. Investigating the causes for the phenomena of nature that are so much a part of our environment and daily routine are the main focus of this major section of the book.

"Peoples of the World" compares the basic essentials of living that are common to all of us, regardless of where on earth we live. Multicultural topics include clothing, language, homes, food, money, crafts and celebrations. These subjects are the focus of the puzzles and activities contained in this section.

There is also a section containing outline maps that can be used by the teacher in a variety of ways according to personal preference. Several suggestions are provided that can be used to determine student proficiency in reading maps.

A Planet in Peril culminates the entire book with a "where-do-we-go-from-here?" theme that gives students food for thought and leaves them with reflections on the future of our planet.

There is a card game, too, that can be used as a review of all terms and concepts that are investigated throughout the book and a complete answer key for teacher convenience.

GA1309

MAP READING SKILLS

PICTURE THIS

When we look at a map we are in reality looking at a picture of part of the earth itself. When we look at a photo we are looking at a much smaller representation of a subject that is out there in the real world. The image produced by the film in the camera creates a nearly perfect idea of the subject in our minds. That is why old photos are so treasured by family members and friends. Often the main reason for taking a photograph is to record an event that is frozen in time to be treasured later or to create a mood or aesthetic response in others who view the photo. In this respect, taking pictures is a form of art expression.

A mapmaker, on the other hand, is concerned with creating a picture of a part of the earth that will accurately inform the reader of the precise location of all that is included in the subject.

Look at the picture below and jot down all that you see on the lines to the right.

_____

_____

_____

_____

_____

_____

_____

_____

_____

_____

Assume you have been asked to reproduce the drawing in the frame below. Draw your own version of the subjects in the picture, being as accurate as you can.

How did you identify the various subjects in the picture you drew?

_____

_____

_____

_____

_____

_____

_____

_____

PICTURE THIS

Now look at this picture below and list all that you see on the lines to the right.

_____

_____

_____

_____

_____

_____

_____

_____

_____

_____

The subjects you see in the picture above are the kinds of things that mapmakers represent when they draw maps to portray the real world. Since accuracy is much more important to mapmakers than it was to you in the picture you drew, they resort to symbols that represent subjects in the real world. They must then let the reader know what those symbols represent. The explanation of their meanings is called the *key* or *legend*. In the box below, create your own version of the picture above. Use symbols of your choice, but be as accurate in their placement as you can. Make a key to the right of your picture.

Key

Explain the meanings of your symbols.

_____

_____

_____

_____

_____

GA1309

USING MAP SYMBOLS

When mapmakers create maps, they attempt to show a portion of the real world as accurately as possible, pinpointing the proper locations of the subjects that are included in their representation. To do this, they use symbols that represent the subjects in the real world. For example, a common symbol for charting the location of mountains is the use of the symbol /\/\/\/\ . This symbol can be made simply and shows some relevance toward what it represents in the real world. To be remembered, however, is that this symbol is not universal and has meaning only if it is properly defined in the map key. Below are some other symbols that are sometimes used by mapmakers. Look at each symbol and decide what you think each might represent. Write your response in the blank space beside each symbol. Share your choices with other members of your class.

	Symbol	What Symbol Could Mean
1.		
2.		
3.		
4.		
5.		
6.		

Now try your hand at your own symbols that are simple and easy to draw, but will serve the purpose of depicting the following:

Symbol	What Symbol Could Mean
	School
	Church
	Picnic Area
	Shelter
	Hospital
	Bike Route
	Railroad Crossing

GA1309

USING A COMPASS

We all should be aware that the magnetic needle always points to the north. If you have a compass, it is easy to determine the other directions. Simply face in the direction of the needle and you will be facing to the north. Your back will be facing in a southward direction. If you hold out your arms, your right hand will point to the east, your left hand toward the west. These four directions are called the *cardinal* directions.

Intermediate Directions

Stand beside your desk and face in the direction of north. Hold your arms straight out from your body, and you will be in the same situation as described in the above paragraph.

1. Now move your right arm to a point between where it was and pointing directly in front of you. In what direction would you call this point between north and east?

   _____

2. Now swing your right arm to a point between east and south. What should you call this direction? _____

3. Move your left arm to a point between west and south. What is this direction? _____

4. Move your left arm to a point between north and west. What is this direction?___

These in-between directions are called the *intermediate* directions.

Label the points on the compass to the right.

GA1309

JEFFERSON MIDDLE SCHOOL

The students in the sixth grade social studies class at Jefferson were given the assignment of mapping the neighborhood area around their school. Their purpose in doing this was to demonstrate to their teacher, Mr. Foster, their knowledge of cardinal and intermediate directions in the real world. Armed with only a compass, their notebooks and pencils, the students scattered in all directions to do their "research." In exactly one hour the students returned, compiled their information in small groups and reported the points of identification listed below. Their task was then to map the area they had seen. The only ground rule on this map was to use Jefferson Middle School as the center of the map. Your task is to help them map the area using the information they found. Use the blank map provided by your teacher. You may use symbols to represent various places, but you must tell the reader the meanings of those symbols. It might be a good idea to use a pencil with a large eraser.

The fire station is half a block north of Jefferson.

The town square starts one block north of Jefferson.

The library is on the south side of the square.

The drugstore is on the west side of the square.

The Town House cafe is on the east side of the square.

The Toy Box is on the north side of the square.

The Courthouse stands in the middle of the square.

There are, of course, other buildings lining all four sides of the square.

Memorial Hospital is located two blocks south of Jefferson.

The swimming pool is one block east of Jefferson.

The four town tennis courts are just south of the pool.

The State Research Test Plot is a big field south of the hospital.

Billings' Grain Elevator is one and one-half blocks west of Jefferson.

Bardee's Quik-Stop is two blocks west of Jefferson.

Rolling Hills Golf Course begins just west of Bardee's.

Adams Street runs north and south on the east side of the school.

Jefferson Street runs north and south on the west side of the school.

Walnut Street runs east and west on the south side of the school.

Hill Street runs east and west on the north side of the school.

When you have finished, compare your map with those of your classmates. Do your maps look the same?

GA1309

JEFFERSON MIDDLE SCHOOL

GA1309

WHICH WAY. . .USA?

If you were in the city of Chicago and were asked, "Which way is it to New Orleans?" you would respond, "South." If asked the same question about Miami, you would say, "Southeast," because Miami is both south of Chicago and east of Chicago. New Orleans, on the other hand is pretty much straight south. In both cases you are using Chicago as the point of reference. Your answers to the two questions above were based on **what direction the other city is from Chicago.**

What if Miami had been your point of reference? What direction should you go to get to Chicago? Northwest, of course. Look at the map on the accompanying page and the cities listed below, and decide in each case which of the eight general directions (north, south, east, west, northeast, northwest, southeast and southwest) you would travel from the first to get to the second.

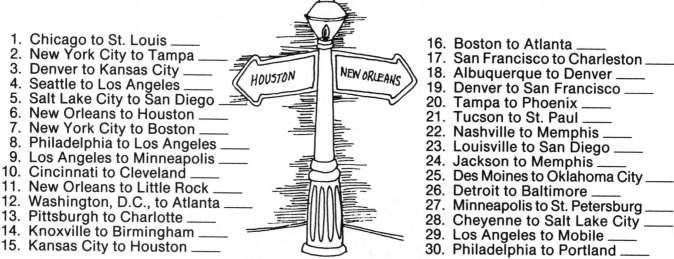

1. Chicago to St. Louis ____
2. New York City to Tampa ____
3. Denver to Kansas City ____
4. Seattle to Los Angeles ____
5. Salt Lake City to San Diego ____
6. New Orleans to Houston ____
7. New York City to Boston ____
8. Philadelphia to Los Angeles ____
9. Los Angeles to Minneapolis ____
10. Cincinnati to Cleveland ____
11. New Orleans to Little Rock ____
12. Washington, D.C., to Atlanta ____
13. Pittsburgh to Charlotte ____
14. Knoxville to Birmingham ____
15. Kansas City to Houston ____

16. Boston to Atlanta ____
17. San Francisco to Charleston ____
18. Albuquerque to Denver ____
19. Denver to San Francisco ____
20. Tampa to Phoenix ____
21. Tucson to St. Paul ____
22. Nashville to Memphis ____
23. Louisville to San Diego ____
24. Jackson to Memphis ____
25. Des Moines to Oklahoma City ____
26. Detroit to Baltimore ____
27. Minneapolis to St. Petersburg ____
28. Cheyenne to Salt Lake City ____
29. Los Angeles to Mobile ____
30. Philadelphia to Portland ____

Now that you are familiar with how to play this game, list twenty more pairs of U.S. cities. Decide which direction the second is from the first. Then test your list with a fellow student while you figure out the directions from his list.

_____   _____

_____   _____

_____   _____

_____   _____

_____   _____

_____   _____

_____   _____

_____   _____

GA1309

WHICH WAY. . .USA?

UNITED STATES

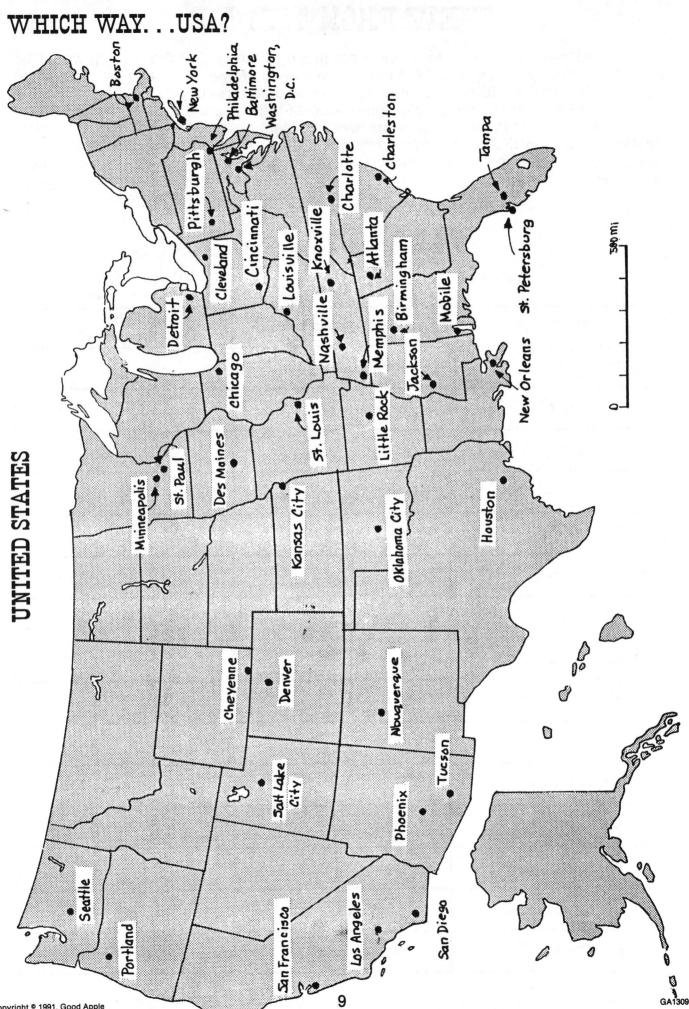

9

VIEW FROM THE TOP

If you could stand on top of the highest mountain in the United States, you would be atop Mt. McKinley in the state of Alaska. If the weather was clear and you looked to the northwest and could see far enough, you could see the city of Fairbanks. That is your assignment in this activity, to imagine yourself high atop some of the world's tallest mountains looking in different directions toward distant places. First, find the mountain's location on a map that shows the surrounding area. Then decide in which direction you would be facing to see the indicated place. On those where a direction is indicated, decide what you would see.

View from. . .	and you could see. . .	you would be facing in the direction of. . .
1. Mont Blanc	the Mediterranean Sea	_____
2. Mt. Olympus	the Aegean Sea	_____
3. Mt. Everest	New Delhi	_____
4. Mt. Aconcagua	Santiago	_____
5. Mt. Rainier	the state capital of _____	west
6. Mt. Whitney	Fresno	_____
7. Mt. Whitney	the city of _____	south
8. Mt. Kilimanjaro	the city of _____	north
9. Mt. Jebel Toubkal (Morocco)	Canary Island	_____
10. Mt. Fuji	Pacific Ocean	_____
11. Mt. Vesuvius	Rome	_____
12. Mt. Kosciusko	the city of _____	northeast
13. Mt. Waddington	Vancouver	_____
14. Longs Peak	Estes Park, Colorado	_____
15. Mt. Shasta	Pacific Ocean	_____

GA1309

NORTH ISN'T UP!

Sometimes young geography students get the mistaken idea that north is "up" . . . south is "down". . .east is "to the right". . .and west is "to the left." They take this mistaken notion with them out into the real world and they become very confused. Such false ideas are no doubt conceived from the fact that most two-dimensional flat wall maps are designed with north pointing toward the top of the paper. But it doesn't have to always be that way! There should always be a compass rose on each map that shows the reader very clearly the directions in the real world that are being portrayed on the map. Look at the example below.

Salamar Island

Answer the following questions:

1. In which direction is the marina from the Seaside Plantation? _____

2. On which side of Salamar Island is the lighthouse? _____

3. Where are the tennis courts from the Seaside Plantation? _____

4. Those staying at the Holiday Hotel will head in which direction when they go to Hillary's?

    _____

5. The Pink Pony is located on which side of Gayle's Gifts? _____

6. The Ocean Breezes Inn is located on which end of Salamar Island? _____

7. To get to the Yogurt Shop from the Holiday Hotel, proceed in which direction? _____

8. Where is the Ocean Breezes Inn from the Drugstore? _____

9. Where is Hillary's from the forest? _____

10. In which direction is the swimming pool from the Seaside Plantation? _____

11

A WALK AROUND TOWN

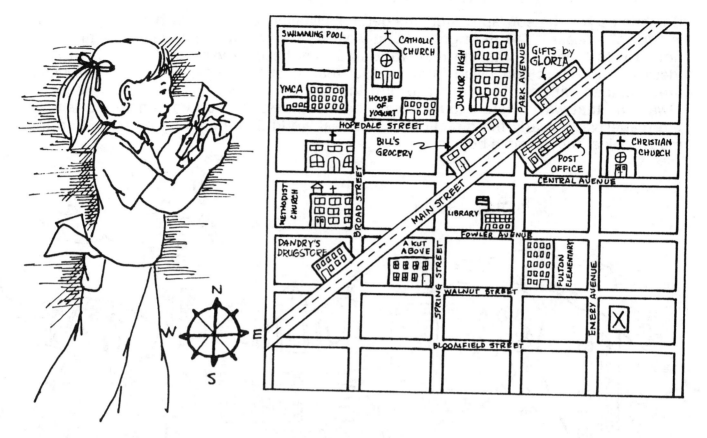

Above is a map of Millidgeville. Assume that you live at 7184 Emery Avenue (marked by the *X*). You have the following lists of "stops" to make on Saturday morning. It's a beautiful day, so you've decided to walk rather than ride your bike. Look at the list. Look at the map, and then decide the order in which you will complete the tasks on your list. Perhaps it would be a good idea to use a pencil with an eraser in case you change your mind.

_____ Take library books back to library.

_____ Mail postcard and bills for Mom.

_____ Take roll of film to camera store for processing.

_____ Make an appointment for racquetball court time at YMCA.

_____ Get haircut appointment at A Kut Above.

_____ Pick up prescription for Mom at Dandry's Drugstore.

_____ Take check to swimming pool to buy summer pass.

_____ Stop for a rest and cup of yogurt at the House of Yogurt.

_____ Practice piano at Christian Church for Sunday's Youth Songfest.

_____ Look for Wendy's birthday present at Gifts by Gloria.

Once you've finished making your choices, exchange your plan with another student and examine together the differences in your plans.

Go back through your list and jot down specific instructions using the directions and a compass to tell someone else how to get from one place on your list to the next.

READING A ROAD MAP

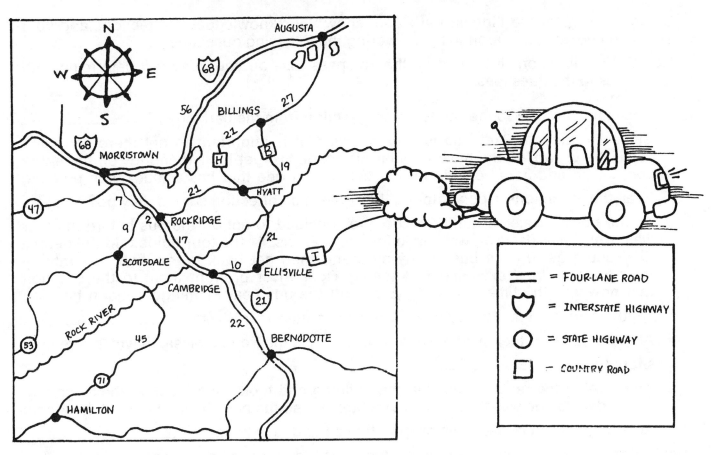

1. What kind of highway is Route 68? _____

2. How far is it from Ellisville to Cambridge? _____

3. What route would you suggest taking in going from Bernodotte to Morristown?

   _____

4. In which direction would you travel in going from Augusta to Rockridge? _____

5. How far is Scottsdale from Hamilton? _____

6. Which route to Hyatt is closer in traveling from Billings? _____

7. In which general direction does Interstate 68 run? _____

8. What routes would you suggest in traveling from Augusta to Bernodotte? _____

   _____

9. How far from Hamilton to Rockridge? _____

10. What river runs through the map? _____

11. According to the legend, what kind of road is Route 71? _____

12. How far is it from Scottsdale to Augusta? _____

13. How far from Morristown to Cambridge? _____

14. Scottsdale to Ellisville is how far? _____

15. How far from Billings to Bernodotte? _____

GA1309

A DAY AT THE ZOO

Using the map of the Lincoln Park Zoo, show your knowledge of directions and your ability to find your way around by answering the following questions.

NOTE: The directions indicated on the compass rose on your map will determine your responses to the questions.

1. The main entrance to the zoo is which direction from the parking lot? _____

2. Since the Lincoln Park Zoo is very crowded, it is important to get there early and "beat the crowd" to the most popular attraction. To get their "bearing" on the entire zoo, Jason and Jarod decide to first take a bus ride that has a tour guide pointing to all the attractions. Upon entering the zoo, which direction should they go? _____

3. As the boys traveled around the zoo, they decided to get off the bus before the tour was over. Their decision was made for two reasons: #1 the tour guide told the people they could get off the bus at any stop and then get back on another to continue their tour; #2 their excitement at seeing Tiger River brought them to the decision that now was the time. As the boys got off the bus near Flamingo Lagoon heading south, in which direction would they head to enter Tiger River? _____

4. After Tiger River, their next adventure was to visit the Reptile Mesa. In which direction should they go? _____

5. After seeing the reptiles, they left the building and took a long look at the alligators. Jason decided he was thirsty and Jarod agreed, so the boys headed toward the Picnic Area to get a soft drink. In which direction should they head? _____

6. Refreshed and ready to see more, the boys waited in a short line to ride the Sky-fari, which was nearby. When they got aboard, they headed in the only direction they could go, which was _____.

7. After a great ride high above the zoo, the boys decided to visit the exhibits immediately to the northwest of the Skyfari where they will see _____.

8. From there, it was time to visit the giraffes, so the boys headed in which direction?

   _____

9. By then it was almost 10:30 and time for the "Predator and Prey" show, which was about to begin in Hunter Amphitheater. As the boys viewed the show, would their eyes be bothered by the sun or not? (It was a very bright sunny day in Lincoln Park.)

   _____

10. After the show, they decided to go into the Rain Forest Aviary, so they headed in what direction? _____

14

GA1309

A DAY AT THE ZOO

11. After the Rain Forest Aviary, Jarod made the statement that he was ". . .hungry and wanted to sit down for awhile." Jason wanted to see more but suggested that they get a sandwich near the lion area so they could eat lunch while they watched the lions. So this is what they did. To get there they headed _____.

12. With lunch out of the way, Jarod wanted to buy another roll of film before they headed out for the afternoon. In which direction should he go to get a fresh roll of film? _____

13. The boys boarded the bus again, this time riding it as far north as it traveled. When they got off the bus, which exhibit did they see? _____

14. From there the boys chose to see the elephants. Again they chose to ride the bus. In which direction will the bus be headed? _____

15. Jason and Jarod left the elephant area and went directly east, where they saw the

    _____.

16. With the afternoon wearing on, they headed for the monkeys. Which way did they go? _____

17. They boarded the bus again and rode across the zoo to the great apes, which meant they were heading _____.

18. The boys then had just enough time to take a couple of "self-pictures" with Jarod's time-release camera in front of the Flamingo Lagoon, which they found by heading

    _____.

19. Jason wanted a T-shirt, which he found in a gift shop which was just _____ of the main entrance.

20. Jason's mother was supposed to pick the boys up at the south edge of the parking lot precisely at 4:00. To get there, Jason and Jarod headed out the main gate and walked in a _____ direction. They were very tired but had spent a wonderful day at a zoo they would never forget.

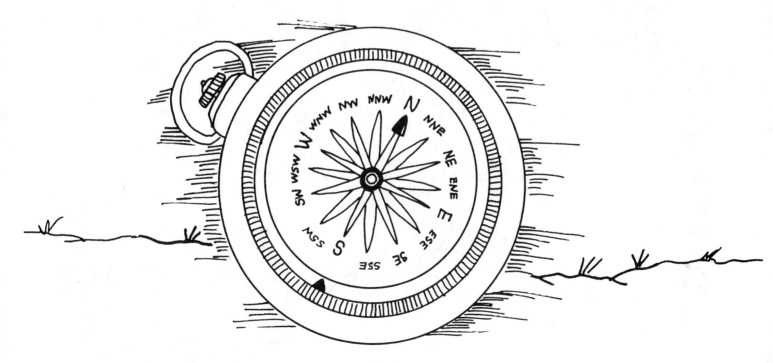

15

GA1309

LINCOLN PARK ZOO

16

MIDTOWN, MONTANA

When it comes to locating particular places on a map, those who make maps use a system that makes it simple for the reader. They use a grid that localizes the search and allows the reader to isolate a specific area of the map. Look at the drawing to the right. Note that the dot (●) locating the city of Hamilton is located within the part of the grid that is called B-2. The horizontal columns in this case are identified by numbers, while the vertical columns are identified with letters. Look at the map again. What letter and number would you use to identify the location of Freeport?

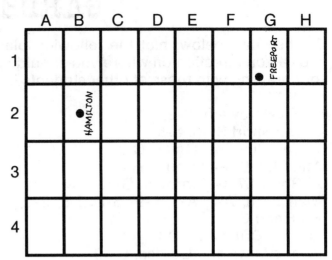

_____

Look at the map below and identify the location of each of these places.

1. ___ Marshall Stadium   5. ___ Monmouth Pottery   8. ___ Midtown City Library
2. ___ Midtown Press   6. ___ Woodrow Wilson School   9. ___ Hancock Co. Hwy. Dept.
3. ___ Presbyterian Church   7. ___ Midtown Lake   10. ___ Picnic Area
4. ___ St. Mary Cemetery

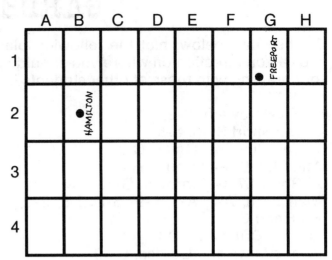

17

GA1309

GARDEN CITY

On the chart below, plot the following places. Use the coordinates that are provided to give you direction on where you should locate each. When you are finished, compare your drawing with those of other students in your class.

Wright Hardware, C-2
Amoco Short Stop, C-5
Garden City Post Office, C-3
Main Street, A-4 through H-4
US Route 67, G-1 through G-10
Swan Lake, A-7, A-8, A-9, B-7, B-8, B-9,
   C-8 and C-9
Sherrick Drugstore, D-2
Casey's Lawn and Garden, C-10

Walnut Street, A-2 through H-2
Madison Street, C-1 through C-10
Fashion Accent, E-4
IGA Grocery, D-4
Garden Apartments, E-2 and F-2
Town and Country Flowers, D-5
Bill's Quik Stop, 7-D

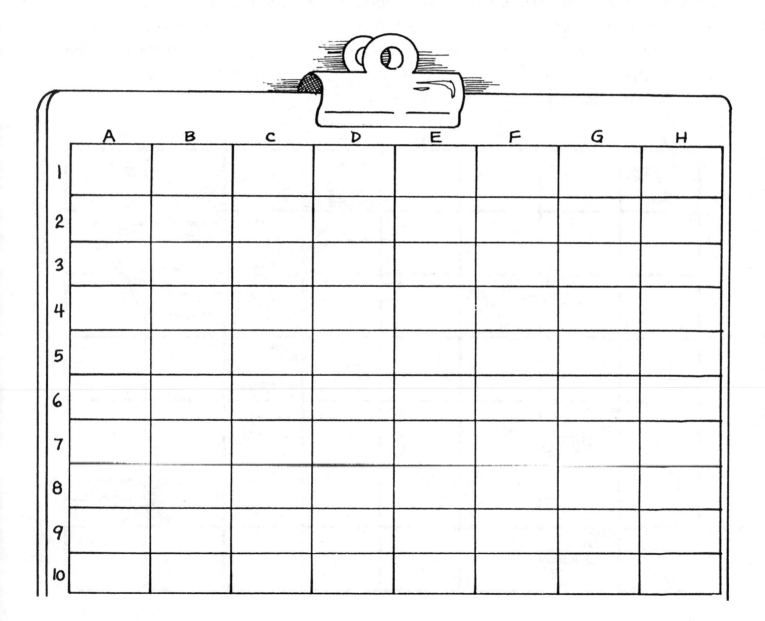

GA1309

PARALLELS

There are imaginary lines on earth that are used in a way very similar to those you used to locate the places in the activity "Midtown, Montana." Some of the lines are horizontal and some are vertical. Used together, they can isolate a specific spot on earth just as you used the letter (vertical) and number (horizontal) lines to locate buildings and places in "Garden City." The horizontal lines are called *lines of latitude*. They are numbered so that those who read maps will know which line is the subject used in pinpointing a particular place.

The point from which lines of latitude are measured is called the *equator*. Label the equator on the globe below and mark it 0^0. The lines of latitude north of the equator are named *north latitude*. They extend all the way to the North Pole, which is 90^0 north latitude. Label both on your map. The lines of latitude south of the equator are named *south latitude*. They extend to the South Pole which is 90^0. Label both on your map. Look at the number of lines remaining on your map and figure out (and label) what they should be called. These lines are called *parallels,* because the distance between a line of latitude and another either north or south of it always remains the same . . . all the way around the earth.

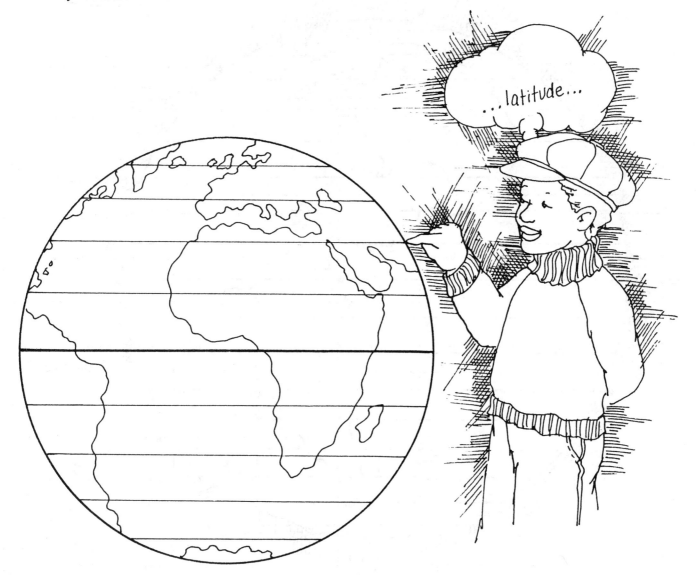

19

NORTHERN OR SOUTHERN HEMISPHERE?

Locate each letter on the drawing below and indicate whether it is in the Northern Hemisphere (N) or Southern Hemisphere (S). Each line on the map represents 10 degrees of latitude. Decide also the number of degrees each point is either north or south of the equator. For example, Point A is north of the equator and is on the line that should be labeled 20⁰, so your answer should be 20⁰ north.

A = _____   F = _____   K = _____

B = _____   G = _____   L = _____

C = _____   H = _____   M = _____

D = _____   I = _____   N = _____

E = _____   J = _____   O = _____

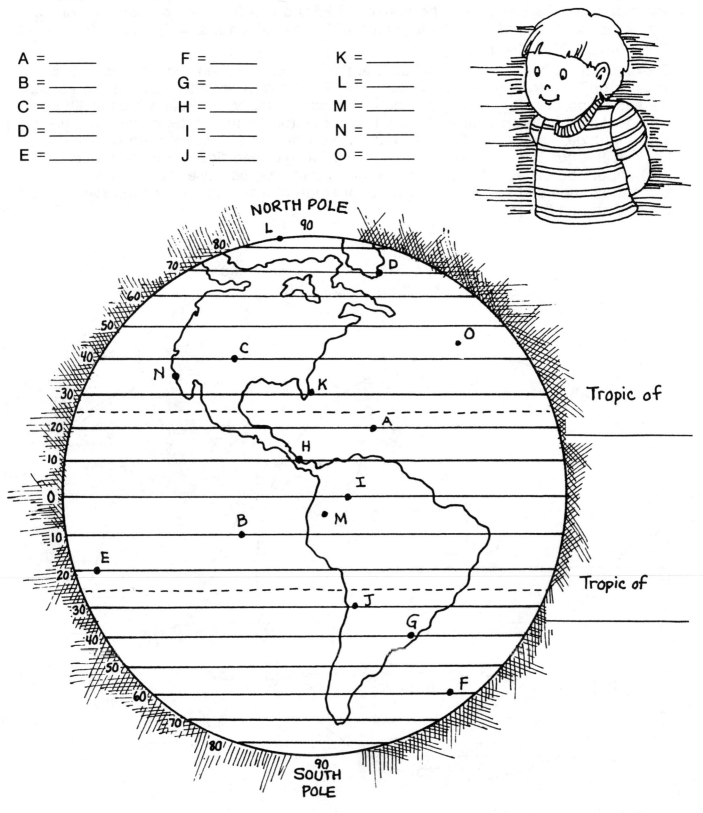

GA1309

MERIDIANS

With the imaginary lines of latitude spanning the earth horizontally, there are also imaginary lines running vertically around the earth. These lines are called *meridians* or *lines of longitude*. Unlike the parallels which always remain the same distance from other parallels, lines of longitude meet or *converge* at the poles. The line from which all other meridians are measured is called the *prime meridian*. It is called 0⁰ longitude. Everything west of the prime meridian to 180⁰ is called *west longitude*, and everything east of the prime meridian to 180⁰ is referred to as *east longitude*.

Lines of longitude are also used in measuring time zones. They can be further used to measure distances, but their most important function is to pinpoint locations on earth when used in conjunction with lines of latitude.

Label the prime meridian and poles on the globe below. Identify those meridians shown west of the prime meridian with the letter *W* to indicate west longitude and those east of the prime meridian with the letter *E* to indicate east longitude. How do you explain that the numbers going in both directions only go to 90⁰?

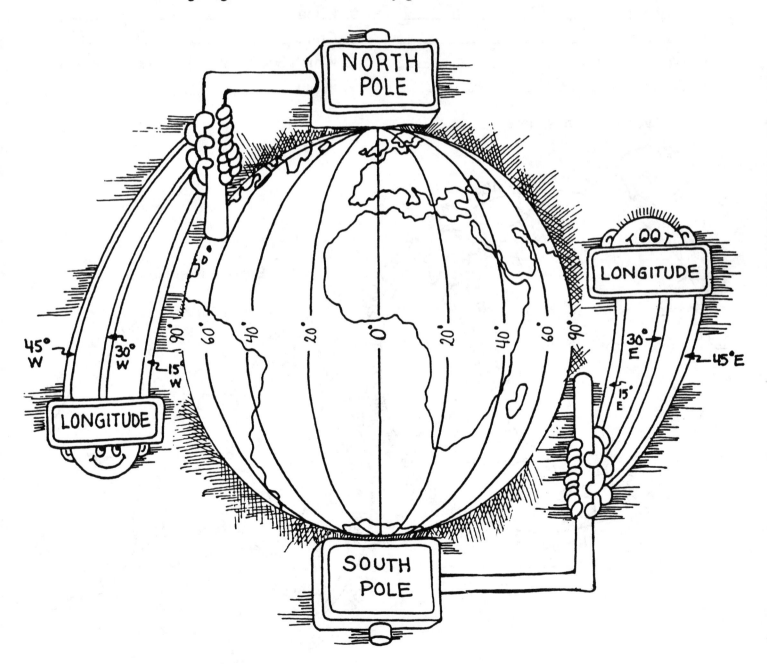

GA1309

THE HEMISPHERES

To review what you have learned thus far: The lines of latitude (parallels) run horizontally around the earth measured from the equator which divides the Northern and Southern Hemispheres. The lines of longitude (meridians) that run vertically and meet at the poles are measured from the prime meridian, which separates the Eastern and Western Hemispheres.

Look at the drawings of the Eastern and Western Hemispheres below and decide in which two hemispheres (east or west, north or south) each of the following is located. For example, we would say the United States is in both the Northern and Western Hemispheres.

1. Soviet Union _____
2. Australia _____
3. Argentina _____
4. Canada _____
5. West Germany _____
6. Costa Rica _____

7. Japan _____
8. Uruguay _____
9. Cuba _____
10. China _____
11. Which two hemispheres have the most land? _____

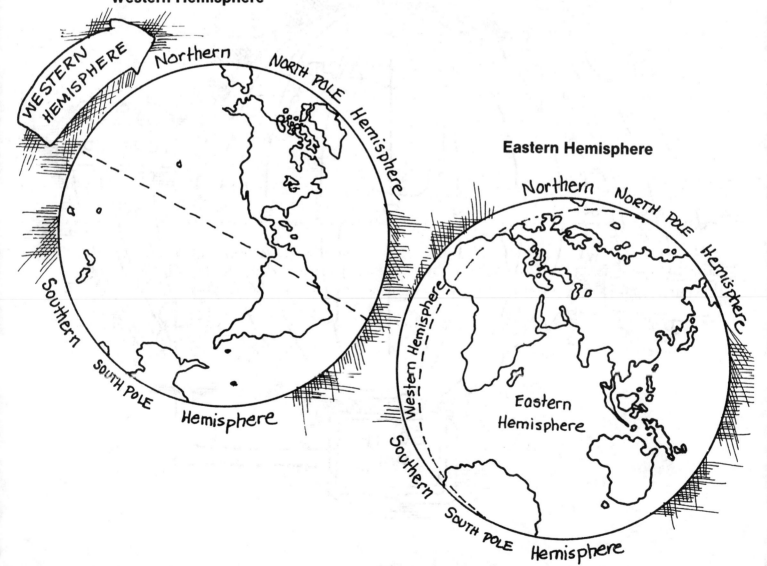

22

GA1309

PINPOINTING MAJOR CITIES

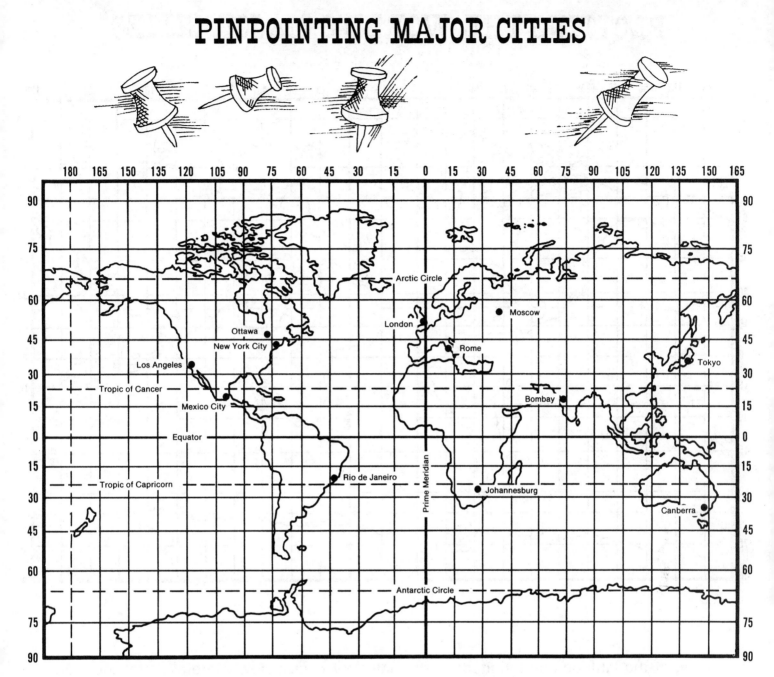

Find each of the cities in the list below on the above map and determine both its latitude and longitude in the blank spaces provided. Be certain to indicate both number of degrees and direction from equator (north or south) and prime meridian (east or west).

City	Latitude	Longitude		City	Latitude	Longitude
1. Moscow	_____	_____		7. Los Angeles	_____	_____
2. New York City	_____	_____		8. Canberra	_____	_____
3. Tokyo	_____	_____		9. Johannesburg	_____	_____
4. Rio de Janeiro	_____	_____		10. Rome	_____	_____
5. Mexico City	_____	_____		11. Ottawa	_____	_____
6. London	_____	_____		12. Bombay	_____	_____

23

GA1309

PLOTTING THE WORLD'S MAJOR CITIES

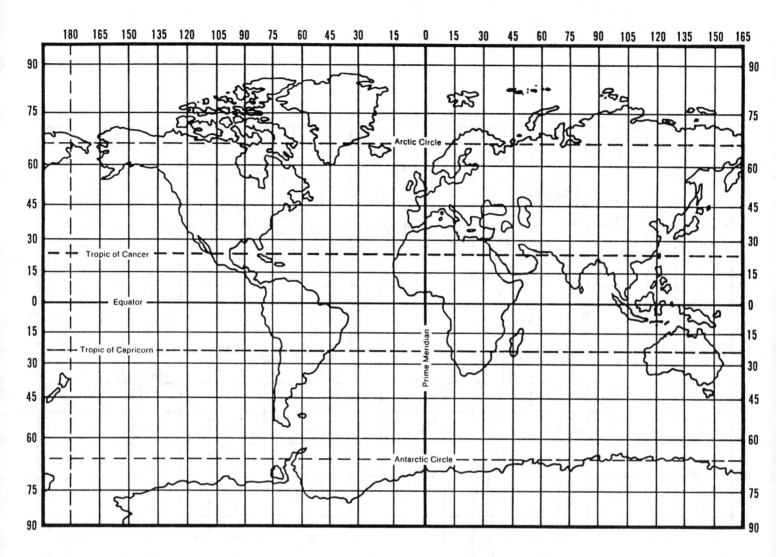

Look at the latitude and longitude coordinates for each below. Carefully plot them on the map above to pinpoint the location of one of the world's major cities. Next try to guess the name of the city you have just located. Finally, check your accuracy with a good map of the world and place the name of the city both on the map and in the blank space provided. How many of your guesses were accurate?

	City	Latitude	Longitude		City	Latitude	Longitude
1.	_____	52° north	13° east	7.	_____	30° north	31° east
2.	_____	40° north	116° east	8.	_____	33° north	117° west
3.	_____	42° north	87° west	9.	_____	44° north	79° west
4.	_____	49° north	2° east	10.	_____	41° south	175° east
5.	_____	34° south	18° east	11.	_____	22° north	114° east
6.	_____	35° south	58° west	12.	_____	10° north	67° west

24

GA1309

CHALLENGE AROUND THE WORLD

For this activity use the accompanying map of the world. Your task is to start at the point given in each situation. Carefully follow the directions in the order in which they are given. As you move your pencil east or west, north or south, you will get closer to the mystery city with each move. When you have completed all the moves, you will have arrived at a spot on earth where a major city is located. To find out what that city is, note the location on your map and compare it with a map or globe that has major cities indicated. Fill in the blank space with the name of the correct city.

1. Start at the prime meridian
   at a point 46⁰ north latitude.

   move 21⁰ south
   move 35⁰ west
   move 20⁰ south
   move 45⁰ west
   move 20⁰ north

   You are at _____ latitude and

   _____ longitude.

   The city is _____.

2. Start at the equator
   at a point 24⁰ east longitude.

   move 20⁰ south
   move 60⁰ east
   move 12⁰ north
   move 30⁰ east
   move 30⁰ north

   You are at _____ latitude and

   _____ longitude.

   The city is _____.

3. Start at 30⁰ south latitude
   at a point 112⁰ west longitude.

   move 22⁰ south
   move 46⁰ east
   move 20⁰ north
   move 52⁰ west
   move 42⁰ north
   move 52⁰ east

   You are at _____ latitude and

   _____ longitude.

   The city is _____.

When given a city, to begin you will need to locate the latitude and longitude of that city before proceeding on with your map work. You will find this information in any good atlas.

4. Start at London

   move 40⁰ east
   move 7⁰ north
   move 56⁰ west
   move 20⁰ south
   move 40⁰ east

   You are at _____ latitude and

   _____ longitude.

   The city is _____.

5. Start at Tokyo

   move 42⁰ east
   move 40⁰ south
   move 41⁰ east
   move 8⁰ north
   move 58⁰ east
   move 40⁰ north

   You are at _____ latitude and

   _____ longitude.

   The city is _____.

6. Start at San Diego

   move 43⁰ west
   move 12⁰ south
   move 23⁰ south
   move 29⁰ west
   move 40⁰ south
   move 20⁰ west
   move 9⁰ north

   You are at _____ latitude and

   _____ longitude.

   The city is _____.

GA1309

CHALLENGE AROUND THE WORLD

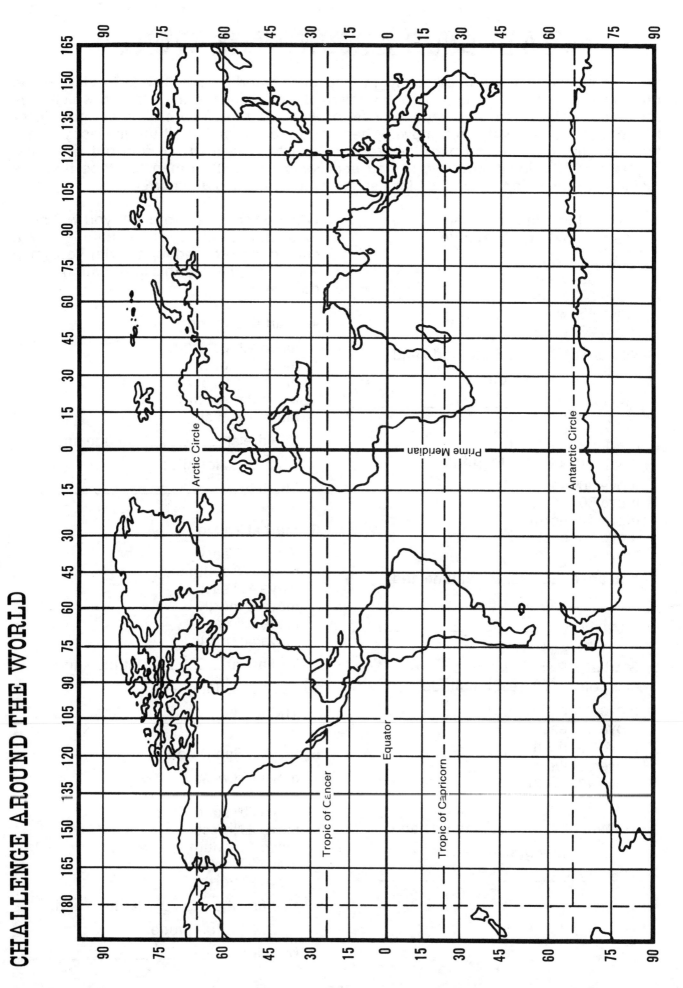

26

MEASURING DISTANCES WITH LATITUDE AND LONGITUDE

The circumference of the earth at the equator is approximately 25,000 miles. This imaginary line called the equator is really just a circle around the earth and thus contains 360 degrees. If you divide 25,000 by 360 you will find that there are approximately 70 miles in distance from one degree in longitude to the next. For example, in the drawing to the right, the distance between 10^0 west longitude (Point A) and 30^0 west longitude (Point B) is 20 degrees. If you multiply those 20 degrees by the 70 miles covered in distance by each degree, you can estimate that the distance between Point A and Point B is approximately 1400 miles.

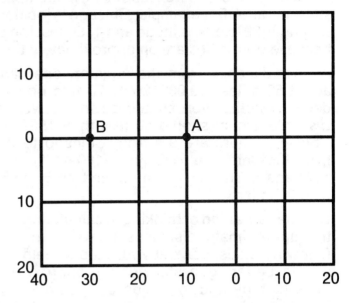

It would be simple if this were the case throughout the earth. The parallels of latitude, however, become shorter in distance as they get closer to the poles. Look at the distances below at the various latitudes.

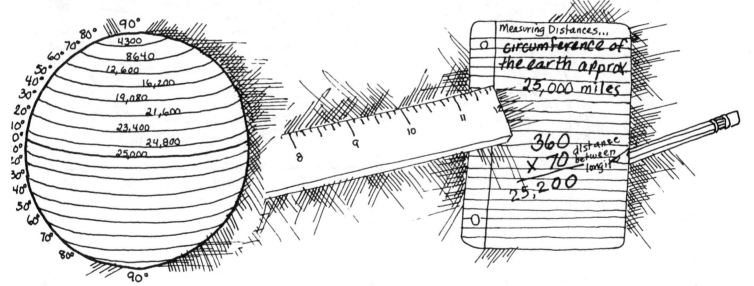

Calculate the approximate number of miles that lie between each degree of longitude at the following parallels. Use the same method you used in calculating the seventy-mile distance at the equator.

0^0 = 70 miles per degree

1. 10^0 = _____

2. 20^0 = _____

3. 30^0 = _____

4. 40^0 = _____

5. 50^0 = _____

6. 60^0 = _____

7. 70^0 = _____

8. 80^0 = _____

GA1309

DISTANCES BETWEEN MAJOR CITIES

Using the information you calculated in the last activity, you can then make some "educated guesses" on about how far apart cities are that are on approximately the same parallel. For example, Chicago is located at 41^0 north latitude and 87^0 west longitude. Beijing is 39^0 north latitude and 116^0 east longitude. We can use this method of calculation because both cities are on approximately the same parallel (41^0 and 39^0).

At that distance from the equator, one can see that each degree of longitude spans about 53 miles ($19,080 \div 360$). To find how many degrees Chicago is from Beijing, first decide whether you should go to the west or to the east. *Always choose the shortest distance*, which should be less than 180^0. In this case, you would go to the west from Chicago. There are 93^0 from Chicago to the international date line ($180-87^0$) and 64^0 from the date line to Beijing ($180-116^0$). Thus Chicago and Beijing are approximately 157^0 apart. That figure multiplied by 53 miles per degree yields an estimated distance of 8321 miles.

Use the same kind of thinking in calculating the approximate distances between the following cities. Look at your map to help you to better "guesstimate" the approximate latitude and longitude of each city. Remember that your estimates are merely that and that the method is the most important thing to be learned in this activity.

Globe diagram with latitude values: 4300, 8640, 12,600, 16,200, 19,080, 21,600, 23,400, 24,800, 25,000

1. Mexico City, Mexico, to Bombay, India	3. Cape Town, South Africa, to Santiago, Chile
2. Chicago to New York City	4. Toronto, Canada, to Bucharest, Romania

GA1309

DISTANCES BETWEEN MAJOR CITIES

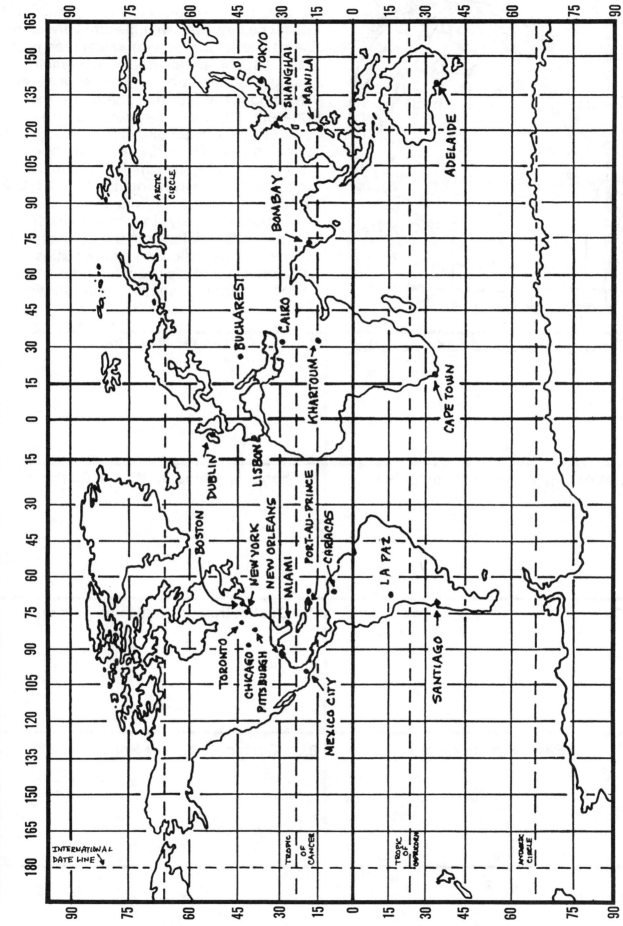

GA1309

CITIES ON THE SAME LONGITUDE

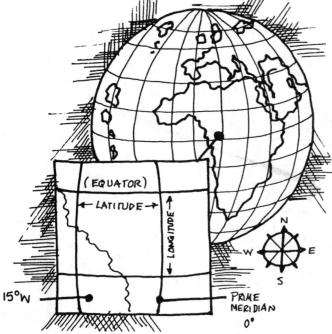

It is a fairly simple task to estimate the distance between two cities that are on the same meridian. First to remember is the fact that the parallels always remain the same distance apart. You should also remember the fact that there are approximately 70 miles between degrees of latitude. For example, this distance between a city that is 38° north and one that is 40° north is approximately 140 miles (70 miles × 2). However for this little trick to work, the cities to be measured *must be* on approximately the same meridian. Calculate the distance in the same manner for each of the following pairs of cities. You will need to find the exact latitudes of each city from another source (atlas, almanac).

1. Tokyo, Japan, to Adelaide, Australia	**5.** **Chicago to New Orleans**
2. Cairo, Egypt, to Khartoum, Sudan	**6. Shanghai, China, to Manila, Philippines**
3. Caracas, Venezuela, to La Paz, Bolivia	**7. Dublin, Ireland, to Lisbon, Portugal**
4. **Pittsburgh to Miami**	**8. Boston to Port-au-Prince, Haiti**

GA1309

LONGITUDE AND THE TIME OF DAY

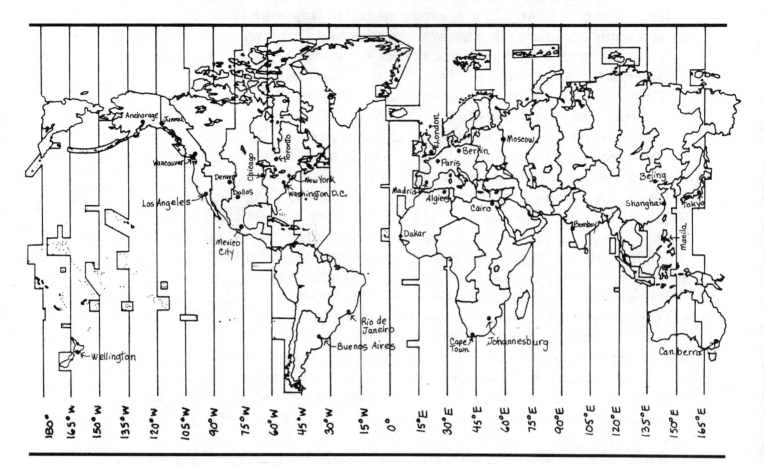

You learned earlier that the earth has a circumference of 360°. You are also aware that there are 24 hours in each day. Understanding a few other basic facts will help you to learn just why our clock/time relationship works the way it does. First, the earth rotates on its own axis, and it takes 24 hours for it to make one complete rotation of this cycle. Thus, at whatever time it is precisely as you read this, it will be 24 hours from now before the spot on the earth where you are located will be in the same position in relationship to the sun.

Next, since there are 360° in the circumference of the earth. . .and since there are 24 equal segments of time (hours) that pass during each rotation of the earth on its axis, it follows that 15° of longitude are spanned by each hour. Thus looking at the map, you can see that the time changes one hour for each 15°.

Finally, the earth rotates on its axis in a west to east direction, moving toward the sun. This makes our day begin with the sun "rising" to the east and "setting" in the west. Look at the map and count the number of time zones there are between New York City and London. If you counted five time zones, you were correct. Thus if it is 1:00 p.m. in New York City, what time is it in London? On the other hand, if it is 3:00 p.m. in London, what time is it in New York City?

31

GA1309

COMPARING TIME ZONES

1. How many hours are there between New York City and Anchorage, Alaska? _____
   If it is 3:00 p.m. in Anchorage, what time is it in New York City? _____
2. How many hours are there between London and Moscow? _____
   If it is 6:00 p.m. in Moscow, what time is it in London? _____
3. How many hours are there between Manila and Bombay? _____
   If it is 11:00 p.m. in Bombay, what time is it in Manila? _____
4. How many hours are there between Paris and Tokyo? _____
   If it is 1:00 p.m. in Paris, what time is it in Tokyo? _____
5. How many hours are there between Chicago and Cairo? _____
   If it is 8:30 p.m. in Chicago, what time is it in Cairo? _____
6. How many hours are there between Los Angeles and Canberra, Australia? _____
   If it is 9:00 p.m. in Canberra, what time is it in Los Angeles? _____
7. How many hours are there between Washington, D.C., and Dallas, Texas? _____
   If it is 12:15 a.m. in Washington, D.C., what time is it in Dallas? _____
8. How many hours are there between Beijing and Johannesburg? _____
   If it is noon in Beijing, what time is it in Johannesburg? _____
9. How many hours are there between Toronto and Rio de Janeiro? _____
   If it is 2:00 a.m. in Rio de Janeiro, what time is it in Toronto? _____
10. How many hours are there between Denver and Mexico City? _____
    If it is 11:15 p.m. in Mexico City, what time is it in Denver? _____
11. How many hours are there between Johannesburg and New York City? _____
    If it is 7:00 a.m. in New York City, what time is it in Johannesburg? _____
12. How many hours are there between Tokyo and Berlin? _____
    If it is midnight in Tokyo, what time is it in Berlin? _____
13. How many hours are there between Rome and Mexico City? _____
    If it is 6:30 p.m. in Mexico City, what time is it in Rome? _____
14. How many hours are there between Vancouver and Rio de Janeiro? _____
    If it is 7:00 p.m. in Vancouver, what time is it in Rio de Janeiro? _____
15. How many hours are there between Dakar and Bombay? _____
    If it is 4:00 a.m. in Bombay, what time is it in Dakar? _____
16. How many hours are there between Buenos Aires and Moscow? _____
    What time is it in Buenos Aires when it is midnight in Moscow? _____
17. How many hours are there between London and Denver? _____
    At 3:30 p.m. in London, what is the correct time in Denver? _____
18. How many hours difference are there between Madrid and Manila? _____
    When it is 8:00 p.m. in Manila, what time is it in Madrid? _____
19. How many hours difference are there between Mexico City and Johannesburg?
    _____
    If it is 2:00 p.m. in Johannesburg, what time is it in Mexico City? _____
20. How many hours difference are there between New York City and Tokyo? _____
    When it is 10:00 p.m. in Tokyo, what time do the clocks read in New York City?

CALIFORNIA

NEW YORK

GA1309

CHANGING TIMES

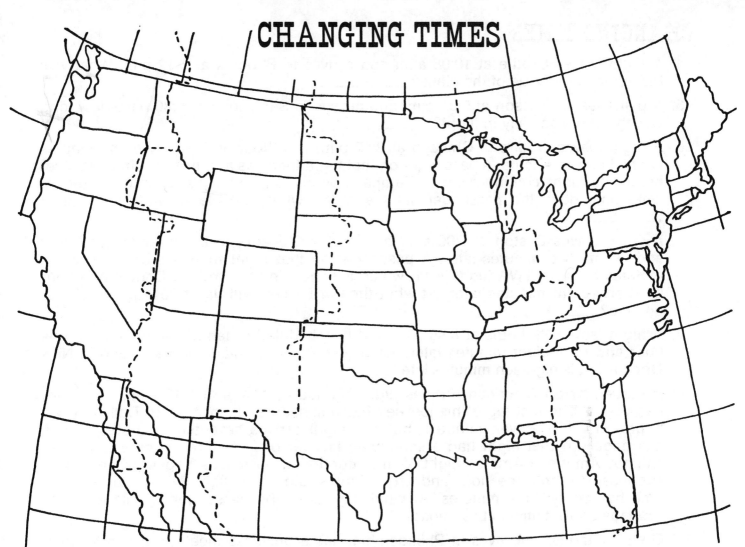

Above is a map of the time zones in the United States. If you include Alaska and Hawaii, a total of six time zones span the United States. The map above shows only the four zones that cover all but those two states. In each of the situations below, decide first which time zone is involved, then how many hours there are between them and finally how much real time passes during the flight.

1. A plane leaves Chicago at 1:12 p.m. for New York. The flight lasts one hour and fifty-two minutes. If the plane arrives on time, at what time should the passenger set his watch when the plane lands? _____

2. A plane leaves from Philadelphia at 8:35 a.m. It arrives at its destination in Kansas City two hours and fourteen minutes later. What time is it in Kansas City when the plane arrives? _____

3. A passenger leaves on a flight out of Cedar Rapids, Iowa, at 6:44 a.m. It lands in Moline, Illinois, to pick up additional passengers and moves on to St. Louis, Missouri, where it lands for a total trip time of one hour and fifty-six minutes. In St. Louis, Nancy Marquez (who was a passenger on the flight) has thirty-five minutes to catch flight 203 for San Diego. That flight will last four hours and two minutes. If the plane arrives on schedule in San Diego, at what time should Nancy set her watch to have the correct "local" time upon arrival? _____

33

CHANGING TIMES

4. A flight leaves Seattle at 10:08 a.m. and arrives in Phoenix at 1:12 p.m. What was the actual flying time of the plane? _____

5. A plane leaves Tucson at 5:32 p.m. and arrives in San Diego at 5:30 p.m. How long was the plane actually in flight? _____

6. A flight leaves O'Hare in Chicago at 2:12 p.m. One hour and twenty-eight minutes later it lands in Atlanta. A passenger on that flight then has a forty-five-minute layover before its flight continues on to Tampa, where it lands forty-six minutes later. At what time does the passenger set his watch when the plane lands in Tampa? _____

7. A plane leaves Boston at 7:06 a.m. headed for Chicago, where it lands two hours and twenty-two minutes later. A passenger on that flight then has only thirty-five minutes to catch TWA flight 2011, which is scheduled to arrive in Denver one hour and forty-eight minutes later. At what time in Denver will flight 2011 arrive, if it is on time? _____

8. A flight leaves St. Louis at 8:45 a.m. and is scheduled to land in New Orleans one hour and forty-eight minutes later. What time does the plane actually land in New Orleans if it is eighteen minutes late? _____

9. A passenger on American Airlines flight 706 leaves Miami at 8:15 a.m., bound for Las Vegas. The first leg of his journey has a scheduled flight time to Dallas of two hours and thirty-seven minutes, but the flight arrives seventeen minutes late. A passenger on that flight had a scheduled layover of forty-three minutes. He then catches American Airlines flight 82 that continued on to Las Vegas, where it was supposed to land one hour and fifty minutes later. But flight 82 is also late, this time by twenty-three minutes. At what time does the passenger set his watch to have the correct time in Las Vegas? _____

10. G.W. Timmons, who lives in Philadelphia, has a business meeting in Los Angeles scheduled for 2:00 p.m. at a conference room in a hotel near the airport. He catches a plane in Philadelphia at 8:06 a.m. on a flight to Chicago that lasts one hour and forty-seven minutes. He has a scheduled thirty-five-minute layover in Chicago before catching another flight on to Los Angeles. However, his plane is delayed in taking off, and he arrives in Chicago just five minutes before his connecting flight departs. Timmons races to Gate 46. . .but too late. . .and too bad for Timmons! Flight 114 has just left the ground. . .on time! The next flight leaves in another hour and five minutes. The airline officials place Timmons on the flight. . .which leaves on time for a four hour and two-minute flight. Flight 1028 (Timmons' new flight) arrives twelve minutes ahead of schedule. How much time does Timmons have to get out of the airport, get to the hotel and prepare himself for this all-important meeting? _____

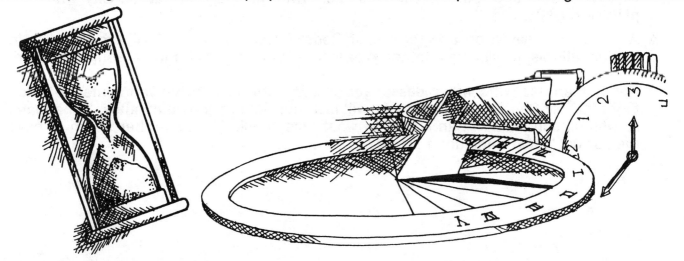

34

GA1309

CHANGING TIMES

Pinpoint the location of each of these cities on your map. Then assume it is 1:00 p.m. in Chicago. In the blank space beside each, indicate the proper local time and provide the identification letters that are used for its time zone. Assume also that it is summer, so daylight saving time is being used.

1. _____ New York
2. _____ Phoenix
3. _____ Seattle
4. _____ Nashville
5. _____ Cleveland
6. _____ Baltimore
7. _____ Detroit
8. _____ Salt Lake City
9. _____ Portland
10. _____ Santa Fe

11. _____ St. Louis
12. _____ Houston
13. _____ New Orleans
14. _____ San Francisco
15. _____ Denver
16. _____ Dallas
17. _____ Philadelphia
18. _____ Kansas City
19. _____ Memphis
20. _____ Tucson

21. _____ Miami
22. _____ Atlanta
23. _____ Las Vegas
24. _____ Minneapolis
25. _____ Los Angeles
26. _____ Boston
27. _____ San Diego
28. _____ Pittsburgh
29. _____ Raleigh
30. _____ Tampa

What time is it right now in. . .

_____ Bangor, Maine
_____ Albuquerque, N.M.
_____ Corvallis, Oregon
_____ Little Rock, Ark.

_____ Orlando, Florida
_____ Charleston, S.C.
_____ Madison, Wisconsin
_____ Shreveport, Louisiana

_____ Boise, Idaho
_____ Birmingham, Alabama
_____ Lincoln, Nebraska
_____ Cheyenne, Wyoming

GA1309

INTERNATIONAL DATE LINE

Exactly 180⁰ in either direction from the prime meridian is the international date line. It is an imaginary line where each day begins. The earth *rotates* on its axis in a west-to-east direction. For this reason, each day is born on the date line and progresses to the west. Thus when crossing the line to the west, one advances one full day. When crossing to the east, one full day is lost.

Decide in each of the situations below the time, whether it is a.m. or p.m., the day of the week and the date. You will need to use the same map used when you compared world time zones.

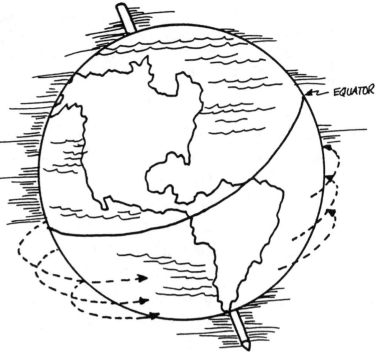

EQUATOR

1. If it is 12:00 noon in New York City on Saturday, July 3, what time is it in London?

   _____

2. When it is the same time in New York as in #1, what time is it in Tokyo?

   _____

3. Considering it is still the same time in New York, what time is it in Johannesburg?

   _____

4. If it is 11:00 a.m. on Friday, October 13 in Tokyo, what is the time in Berlin?

   _____

5. If it is in the same time in Tokyo, what time is it in San Francisco?

   _____

6. If it is 8:00 a.m. on Monday, December 1 in Tokyo, what time is it in Paris?

   _____

7. If it is 7:00 a.m. Wednesday, June 2 in Manila, what time is it in Chicago?

   _____

8. If it is 1:00 p.m. on Thursday, May 12, in Mexico City, what time is it in Melbourne?

   _____

9. If it is 12:00 noon on Saturday, November 12, in Beijing, what time is it in Toronto?

   _____

10. If it is 1:00 p.m. on Wednesday, January 4 in Rio de Janeiro, what time is it Melbourne?

   _____

GA1309

NIGHT AND DAY

To understand why we have night and day on the earth, it is important that you understand the concept of the earth's rotating on its own axis. Think for a moment of a child on a merry-go-round. The pole, or axis, is located in the center with the merry-go-round rotating around and around on that axis. The children who ride are in a similar position to our position in "riding" the earth as it rotates on its axis one complete cycle each twenty-four-hour day.

It is likewise important to understand the reason for those who live east of where we are seeing the sun rise in the morning and set in the evening before we do. Those who live west of us experience both *after* we do. The reason for this phenomena is that the earth spins in a west-to-east direction. Stated another way, the earth rotates on its axis in a counterclockwise direction.

Show your knowledge of the concept of night and day in the space below by drawing the planet Earth and sun as well as using directional arrows and labels in any way you like that will make your explanation clear.

Draw your explanation below.	Write an explanation of your drawing in the space below.

WHERE BEDTIME NEVER COMES

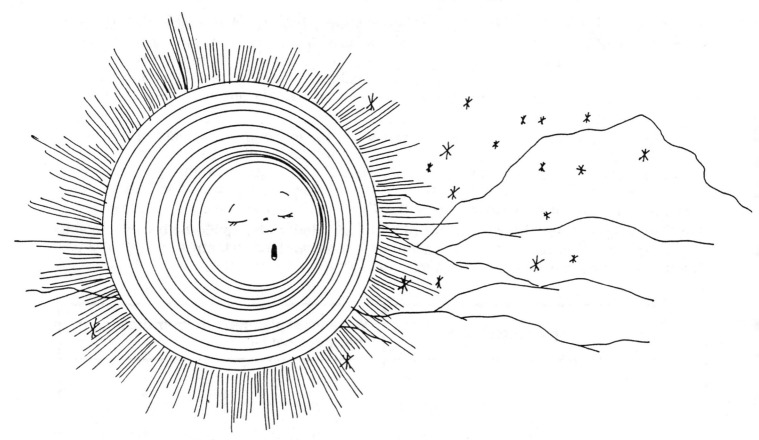

Most of us associate nighttime and darkness with eventually going to sleep. However, there are places on earth where at times darkness never comes. In much of Alaska and other parts of the north, the summer solstice—June 22—brings twenty-four hours of daylight and one of the year's most celebrated times. In fact the sun comes up around May 11 and doesn't truly disappear until around August 3. Even as far south as Anchorage, the twilight lasts all night, even though the sun sets for three to four hours.

North of the Arctic Circle, in communities like Barrow and Wainwright, residents in summer hunt and fish and work and play all day. Recreation may begin after dinner and softball and volleyball games are common at 2 a.m. Children talk to each other through the night on their citizens band radios, which is the common form of communication in such communities.

While twenty-four hours of daylight are cause for celebration by most who live in such places, they present problems for others. One former resident reported, "I found it extremely difficult to get a good night's sleep. All the noise and light just wouldn't allow me to go to sleep." He finally moved back to Virginia, where he had originally lived. Most of us who live in places where the seasons are distinct enjoy summer because it brings to us warmer weather and more sunlight. But twenty-four hours of sunlight? If you did live in such a place, how would you plan your "day"?

Remember, you would have to sleep some time. What other differences in life-style would be required to live in such a place?

GA1309

WHERE BEDTIME NEVER COMES

In the space below, outline how a typical day (twenty-four hours of daylight) would be spent by you.

_____

_____

_____

_____

_____

The dark side of living north of the Arctic Circle is that there is an equal time during the winter months when there is no sunlight. What problems would this present for you if you lived in such a place? Would you like it? Would a summer of daylight be worth the trade-off of a winter filled with dark days? Explain your feelings below.

_____

_____

_____

_____

_____

Such extended periods of darkness often result in people becoming depressed and frustrated. Scientists call it SAD (Seasonal Affective Disorder). Some of the rest of us call it _cabin fever_. Have you ever felt such frustration during times of bad weather? What are some ways to overcome these times of negative and depressed feelings? Have you ever experienced cabin fever yourself?

_____

_____

_____

_____

_____

Contrast this with what scientists call SES (Summer Energy Syndrome), periods of euphoria people sometimes experience when they have more energy and require less sleep than normal. Such periods usually occur during the summer months. Have you ever felt these sudden bursts of energy? How would you explain such instances?

_____

_____

_____

_____

GA1309

OUR CHANGING YEAR

While the earth is constantly rotating on its own axis to give us day and night (as we learned earlier), it is also revolving around the sun. This revolving of the earth is part of the reason we have seasons. It takes 365¼ days for the planet Earth to make one complete revolution in its orbit around the sun. The other part of the reason we have winter and summer is the fact that the earth is tilted on its own axis at an angle of 23½ degrees.

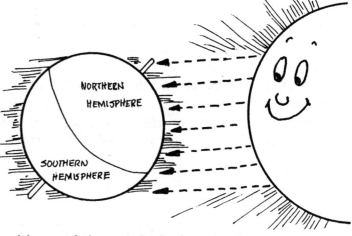

Look at the drawing to the right. Notice that the position of the earth makes the sun's rays shine directly on the Northern Hemisphere. When this happens, we have summer. Notice also that the rays hitting the earth in the Southern Hemisphere are less direct. When this happens, the Southern Hemisphere is experiencing winter. Because the earth continues to change its position relative to the way the sun's rays strike the earth (as it revolves around the sun), we have four seasons.

In the drawing below are shown the four positions of the earth during the four seasons. Label each season as it would appear in the Northern Hemisphere. Also label each globe's season in the Southern Hemisphere. Use any labels or additional drawings or explanation you need to explain the concept of why we have seasons.

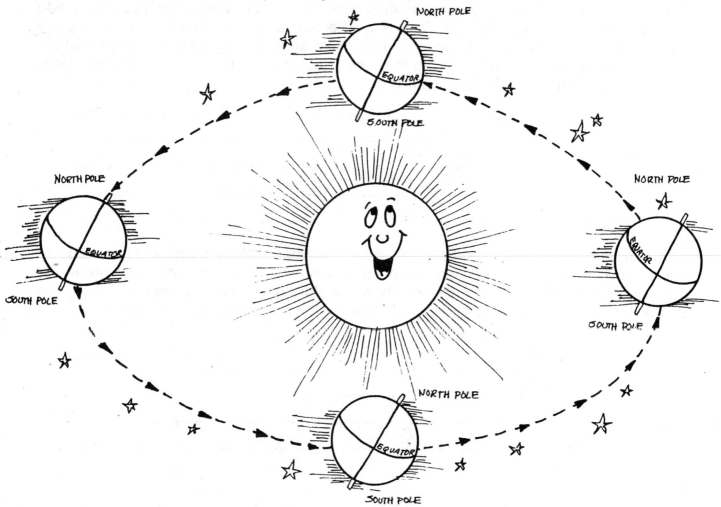

GA1309

GEOGRAPHY CONCEPTS AND DEFINITIONS

GA1309

CLOUDS

Even though clouds vary a great deal in their visible appearance because of color and shape, they are all made up of tiny water droplets or ice crystals. Both are without color, but they appear to be white because they diffuse or scatter sunlight. Clouds are formed whenever the air cools below its dew point. The dew point is the temperature at which the air becomes so filled with moisture that its state turns to a visible water vapor. Raindrops are formed from these water droplets. With further cooling, the water particles grow together and fall as rain. If the atmosphere is cold enough, the droplets become ice crystals.

Various cloud formations have different meanings and are often helpful in predicting upcoming weather patterns. Many years ago British biologist Luke Howard classified clouds into three main groups: *cirrus*, *stratus* and *cumulus*. Your task is to research each from another source and jot down an identifying statement for each as well as to create a drawing in each box that shows what each cloud formation looks like.

Cirrus

Stratus

Cumulus

GA1309

CLOUDS

From these three basic cloud groups, there are other clouds in the sky that bear significance in our day-to-day weather patterns.

Identify each of the following with a short statement:

Cumulonimbus _____

_____

Cirrostratus _____

_____

Nimbostratus _____

_____

Stratocumulus _____

_____

Stratus _____

_____

1. If you wanted to go on a picnic, which of these clouds would you rather see in the sky—cirrus, stratus, nimbostratus? _____

2. Why? _____

3. Which would you least like to see? _____

4. Why? _____

Create your own weather forecast for the United States in the space below. Use names of various cloud formations for different parts of the country that will be "typical" for the kind of weather expected on the day you choose.

_____

_____

_____

_____

_____

GA1309

FAULTS

If you crack the shell of a hard-boiled egg, the result will be a number of cracks all over the area you have damaged. The crus† of the earth is somewhat like that. Those cracks in the earth's outermost layer or crust are called *faults*. Whereas the cracks on the egg remain in the same place, the faults in the earth's crust may shift up, down or sideways in relation to the solid rock that is on the other side of the fault.

Breaks in the crust that involve side-to-side or horizontal movement are called *strike-slip faults*. California's San Andreas Fault is an example of a strike-slip fault. Those breaks involving movement up and down are known as *dip-slip faults*.

EGGSHELL EARTH SHELL

The crust or outer layer of the earth is anywhere from five to fifty miles thick. Slow movements along a fault can cause subtle changes that go unnoticed. When the movement is sudden, the result is an earthquake. Beneath this crust is a slushy layer consisting of solid rock mixed with molten rock. The layer varies in thickness in different places. Beneath this layer of slush is a layer that is very hot and solid and approximately 1800 miles (2900 km) in thickness. Below this is a layer of very hot liquid metal, and at the very core is an area of hot solid metal. This center is extremely hot because of all the pressure that is on it.

Dip-Slip Fault

Strike-Slip Fault

GA1309

FAULTS

. . .For research and further development, choose two of the following:

Most scientists agree that the earth's crust is made of plates that move slowly. What they aren't certain of is how many plates there are, nor just where the edges of the plates are. Find out the names and locations of the eight plates, and draw a rough map of the earth that shows where these faults are located.

Find out how volcanoes are born and what causes them to erupt. Summarize your findings with explanations and drawings.

Describe how an earthquake begins at the focus and expands to the point where it reaches the earth's surface. Include in your explanation terms like *seismic waves* and *epicenter* to show your knowledge and understanding of how an earthquake really happens.

Find out about the Ring of Fire. Make a rough drawing of its location and explain what it is and why the earth is so unstable in this area.

Find out about the Richter scale that is used to measure the intensity of earthquakes. How does it work? What do the numbers mean? What determines catastrophic earthquakes, and what can be done to prevent them from causing such major damage?

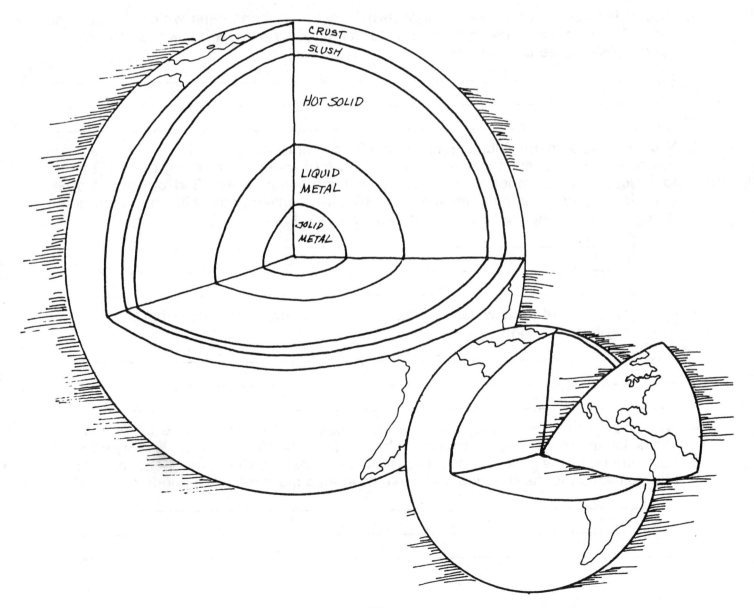

GA1309

DROUGHTS

Drought occurs when an area suffers from a lack of precipitation over an extended period of time. The longer a drought lasts, the more serious it can become. Droughts sometimes last for years. They affect more people on earth than any other natural disaster. Hundreds of thousands of people die annually of the starvation which follows lengthy periods of drought. Their causes are often complex and beyond the control of man. The shifting of the jet stream and changes in the temperature of the ocean have been causes of long-term drought, but there have also been other factors that have entered into the picture.

1. One of the causes of severe drought in the past is a phenomena which the Spanish call El Niño. Research the origin of this term and describe how it has created drought conditions on several occasions.

   _____

   _____

   _____

2. Man has also sometimes been responsible for causing drought. In his effort to harness power and build dams, there is often an excess of water where the ground is unable to absorb it, while other areas wind up with no water at all. Find out about other occasions where man has intervened for his own convenience, with the result being drought to areas that had water prior to the action of man.

   _____

   _____

   _____

3. Look at the current world water picture, and list specific areas on earth that are suffering from long-term drought.

   _____

   _____

   _____

4. With the current technology and the ingenious mind of man, there are steps that can be taken to combat long-term drought situations. Some are obviously more effective than others. In the space below, discuss those measures which can be taken by man to help overcome the situation and make drought a more tolerable condition.

   _____

   _____

   _____

GA1309

CONTINENTAL DIVIDE

The *Continental Divide* is that stretch of elevated land that determines the direction rivers flow on the opposite sides of a continent. The divide usually follows a mountain range that's in a north-south direction.

In North America the Continental Divide follows a path through the Rocky Mountains of Western United States. All river systems lying east of the Rockies flow in the direction of the Atlantic Ocean or the Gulf of Mexico. All rivers west of the Divide flow toward the Pacific.

In the outline maps of the continents below, draw in the path that you think the Continental Divide follows and indicate with arrows the direction of the flow of rivers on either side. Finally label the bodies of water into which these major river systems will flow.

GA1309

CONTINENTAL DRIFT

During the early part of the twentieth century, a theory was advanced by a German scientist that helped to explain the current position of the continents on earth. His theory was based on the similarities of the coasts of South America and Africa, and he concluded that they had at one time been connected as a part of a giant land mass that contained all of the continents. His theory was not widely accepted by others, but over the years, evidence has emerged to give a great deal of support for this theory. Studies of geologic formations, biologic similarities and the sea floor of the oceans have all added to the growing body of evidence that the continents were at one time all connected.

1. Who was the German scientist responsible for the theory of continental drift?

   _____

2. What was the Greek name used to identify the one-time super land mass that included all the continents? _____

3. Find out why molten rock from beneath the earth's crust is changing the position of the continents (according to this theory). _____

   _____

   _____

4. What is *tectonic* activity and what role does it play in this theory? _____

   _____

   _____

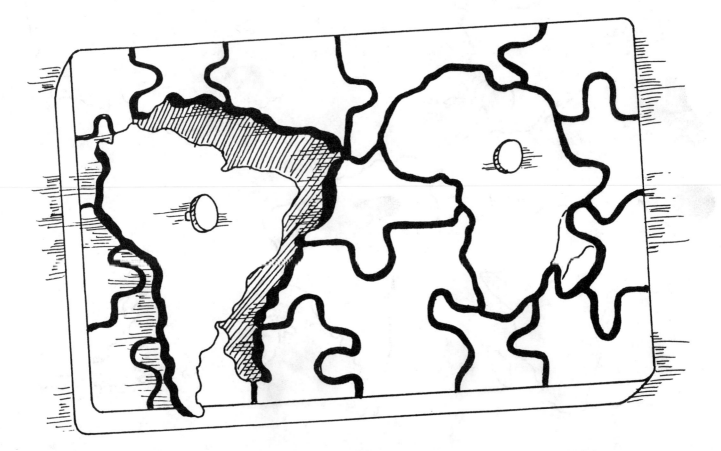

CONTINENTAL DRIFT

Below are outlines of each of the continents. Obtain a sheet of tracing paper and trace the outline of each continent two times. Then cut out the shapes. On another sheet of paper, arrange the continents in the current position and glue them to the paper. Use the other set of patterns to arrange a configuration of the continents the way they may have appeared millions of years ago when they may have been connected. Glue them into position and compare your patterns with those of other students. Discuss both the support and the flaws of the theory.

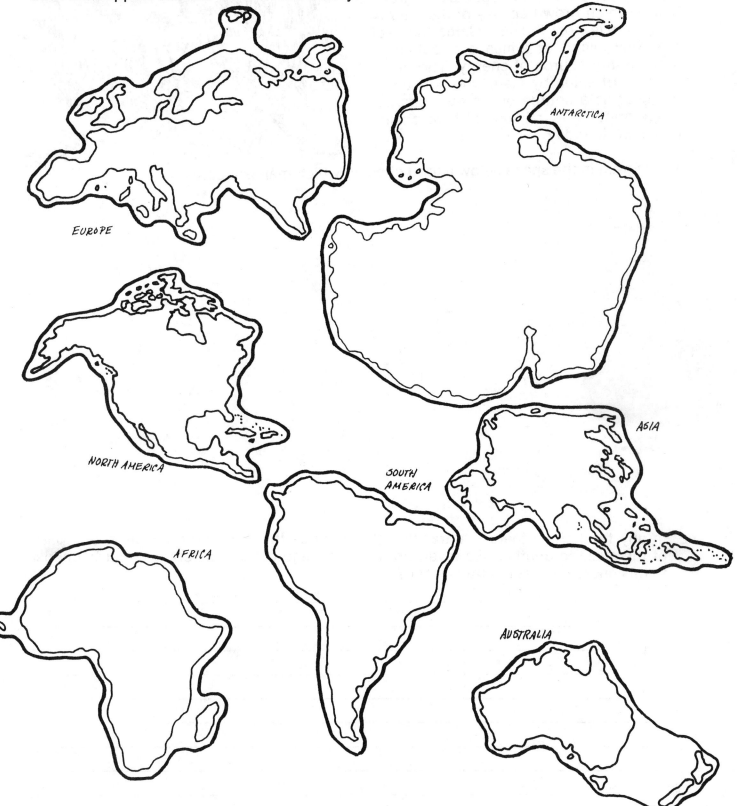

GA1309

FOOD CHAINS

All living things are part of one or a number of food chains. The key ingredient in any one of them is the energy that is passed from one level to the next. The sun provides the main source of energy for virtually all of them. A good example is one in which man is involved. The chain starts with green plants which grow because of the energy they receive from the sun. Cattle then eat the green plants as a means of obtaining a necessary source of energy. The cattle are in turn eaten by man, who consumes the beef as a source of his own energy. There are literally millions of food chains in our world today.

1. Diagram in the space below a food chain in which man is a part.

2. In any food chain there is a transfer of energy as the food is moved from one part of the cycle to another. However, not all of the energy is transferred. What happens to this energy that is not transferred?

_____

_____

_____

_____

_____

_____

_____

_____

GA1309

FOOD CHAINS

3. Describe what happens in a food chain that begins with the remains of dead plants. What are the forces involved in returning such matter back into a food chain?

_____

_____

_____

_____

4. Diagram and describe a typical food chain in which each of the following is involved:

a catfish—

a person living in Japan—

wheat—

51

GA1309

LATITUDE/LONGITUDE

Lines of *latitude* and *longitude* are the imaginary lines around the earth that were created to give people a way of identifying and locating a specific point on earth. They do this by intersecting with each other to form a grid. Lines of latitude are horizontal lines that measure distances north and south of the equator. Since the equator is the beginning point from which all others are measured, it is called 0⁰. The latitude of all points north of the equator to the North Pole are called north latitude. The North Pole measures 90⁰ N.

All points south of the equator to the South Pole are called south latitude and the South Pole measures 90⁰ S. Because these lines of latitude always remain the same distance apart, they are called *parallels*.

Lines of longitude are all measured from an imaginary line called the prime meridian. It runs through Greenwich, England; and since it is the point from which all others are measured, it is 0⁰. The longitude of all points east of the prime meridian to a point halfway around the world (180⁰) are called east longitude. All points west of the prime meridian to that same point halfway around the world (180⁰) are called west longitude. That line that is exactly 180⁰ in either direction from the prime meridian is called the *international date line*. Unlike lines of latitude, which are parallel, lines of longitude all converge or meet at the poles and are called *meridians*. Thus while each degree of latitude covers exactly the same distance as all others, the distance spanned by a degree of longitude depends on how far it is from the equator. The greater the distance it is from the equator, the shorter the length of each degree. At the place, where the meridians converge, there is no distance at all!

To give us even greater accuracy in locating points on earth, each degree of latitude and longitude is divided into sixty equal positions called *minutes*. Each minute is divided further into sixty smaller positions called *seconds*.

GA1309

LATITUDE/LONGITUDE

The latitude and longitude of a point on earth together are called its *coordinates*.

On the map below draw in at least five parallels (lines of latitude) and five meridians (lines of longitude). Be certain to label your lines with the appropriate numbers.

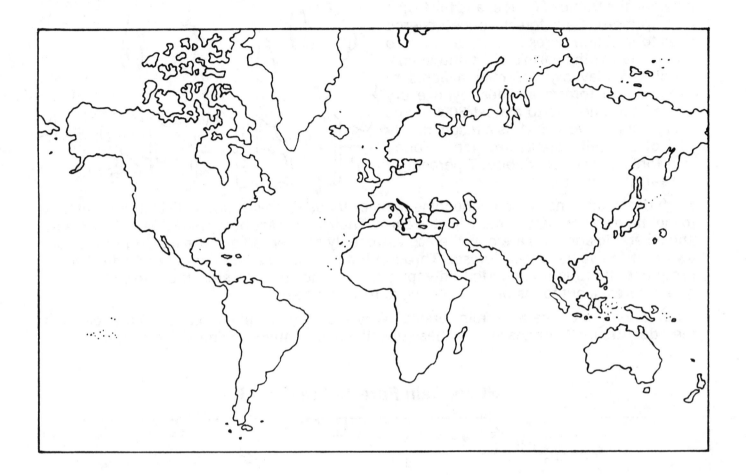

Place an *X* on the spot where you live on the map above. Then find out the exact coordinates of your city or town and place them on the line below.

_____

Place the letter *A* on your map at the point where you think 80⁰ west longitude crosses 20⁰ south latitude.

Place the letter *B* on your map at the point where you think 40⁰ east longitude crosses 60⁰ north latitude.

Place the letter *C* on your map at the point where you think 140⁰ west longitude crosses 35⁰ south latitude.

1. At the equator the distance around the earth is 25,000 miles. At this point of latitude, how many miles would lie between each degree of longitude? (Express your answer to the nearest tenth of a mile.) _____

2. How wide to the nearest hundredth of a mile is one minute? (Each degree is divided into sixty minutes.) _____

3. If each minute spans a distance of approximately 6125 feet, how many feet (to the nearest whole foot) are covered by one second? _____

RAIN FORESTS

Those densely wooded areas found in wet tropical climates are called tropical rain forests. These lands are found in various places throughout the earth in latitudes between the tropic of Cancer and the tropic of Capricorn. Rain forests once covered over four billion acres and were home to almost half of the earth's plant and animal species. Today over 27 million acres of tropical rain forests are destroyed every year. That amounts to almost 3000 acres every hour of every day! As a result, nearly half of our rain forests are gone. Today rain forests cover only about 7 percent of the earth's land area.

Such destruction has recently become a major focus to environmentalists in their efforts to maintain and preserve a more livable earth. Their voices are being heard as governments and scientific agencies are now themselves deeply concerned and are making the people aware of the value of rain forests. Through better land-use techniques and educational programs, there is a concerted attempt going on not only to stop the current decline, of rain forests, but to restore much of what has been lost.

What is the big concern for rain forests? Why are they so valuable and what is causing their destruction? For answers to these questions and others, we must dig deeper.

Where Rain Forests Are Found

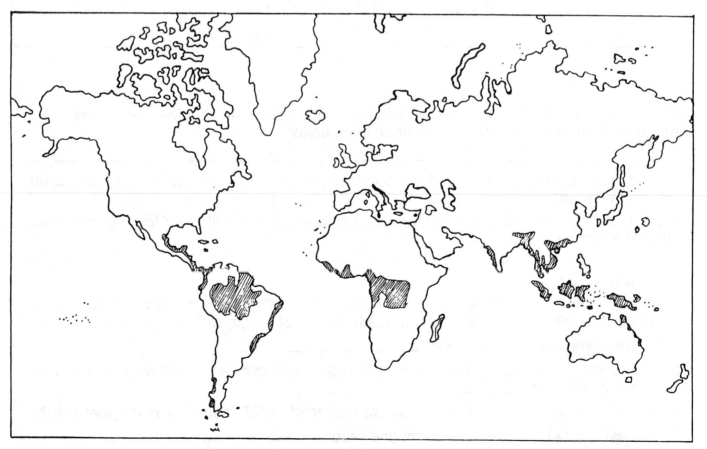

RAIN FORESTS

1. **The Problem Defined:** A rising population combined with a poor economy have caused people to use land once covered by rain forests for agricultural purposes. People are cutting wood for fuel at a rate that far exceeds its ability to grow back. Cattle farmers are clearing huge areas of tropical forests to raise cattle. With a poor economy and a struggle to survive, it is difficult to explain to these people the damage they are causing. Some fast food restaurants are getting their meat from the cattle that are being raised in rain forests. In addition, poor logging practices also contribute to the problem. Once an area is cleared for agricultural purposes, the soil is so poor that it can only sustain life for a short time. Then it's time to move on and cut down more trees. The soil that is left does not restore the forest. That part of the forest is gone. Research the alternatives and describe in the space below what you think can be done.

_____

_____

_____

_____

_____

_____

2. **Why Rain Forests Are Valuable:** Millions of plant and animal species live in tropical rain forests. Some species can only be found there. There are also many valuable medicines and beneficial drugs that are found in the plants that grow in rain forests. They are also an important source of food and fuel to the people who live there. Rubber and wood and several other by-products that are used in our everyday lives come from rain forests. But there is a role perhaps even more significant than these that rain forests play, that being their part in the recycling of the earth's water. Find out about this phenomena and describe in the space below the role played by rain forests. Speculate on what you think will happen if the rain forests are destroyed.

_____

_____

_____

_____

_____

GA1309

ANATOMY OF A RAIN FOREST

Below is a chart that shows the various layers that are found in a rain forest. The first column defines the layers from the top of the forest down. The middle column is left for you to provide a description of the environment found there. The third column provides a space to name some animals that live in each layer.

Layer	Environment	Animals
Emergent layer		
Canopy		
Understory		
Forest floor		
Underground		

Gifts from the Forest: Using a sheet of poster board that measures 22" x 17" (55.88 x 43.18 cm), create a collage of pictures cut from magazines that represents the many gifts that come to us from rain forests. Combine your collage with those of other students to create a "Gifts from the Forest" bulletin board that tells the story of the value of rain forests and what we will lose if someday they are gone.

GA1309

ISLANDS

A body of land that is completely surrounded by water is called an island. Islands are found all over the world. They vary in size from a few hundred square feet to Greenland, the world's largest island of over 800,000 square miles (2.07 million sq. km). It could be said in some sense that the continents themselves are islands because they are surrounded by water. However, for purposes of definition, geographers have classified Greenland and any smaller bodies of land surrounded by water as islands, while Australia (the smallest continent) and all bodies of land that are larger are called continents.

Islands are found in oceans, lakes and rivers in all climates. The land found on the islands themselves can vary from dense tropical jungle to nothing more than barren rock where vegetation is scarce. All islands can be classified by one of the four following methods in which they were found: *oceanic, continental, barrier, coral.* Find out about their differences and describe briefly how each island is formed.

Oceanic _____

_____

_____

_____

Continental _____

_____

_____

_____

Barrier _____

_____

_____

_____

Coral _____

_____

_____

_____

Go back to the list above and name an island that was formed in each of the above ways.

Islands have sometimes provided explorers with some very interesting discoveries because of the strange and unique plant and animal life that has been found. Speculate on how you think such phenomena might have come to happen. (An example might be the giant tortoises of the Galápagos Islands.)

_____

_____

_____

                    GA1309

LAKES

A body of water that is completely surrounded by land is called a *lake*. Lakes that are small in size are called ponds. There are lakes all over the world in various sizes, shapes and depths. Lakes are also found at all altitudes from below sea level (the Dead Sea) to over 17,000 feet (5180 m) above sea level (Panch Pokhri on Mount Everest). Lakes are either open or closed. Those lakes which have water that leaves by way of outlets are called open lakes. These which have no outlets are called closed lakes. Lakes that are open usually contain fresh water and those that are closed are usually saltwater lakes.

Lakes are formed in a variety of ways, most of which are the result of the forces of nature. Some lakes, however, are the result of the digging and damming up by man.

1. Find out how each of the following lakes was formed and briefly explain.

Caspian Sea _____

_____

Great Lakes _____

_____

Lake Mead _____

_____

List other ways in which lakes are created. _____

_____

_____

_____

2. Lakes are in a constant state of change that is all a part of the life cycle of a lake. Those changes are not usually visible to us as they occur over a long period of time. Explain in the space below the stages in the life cycle of a lake.

_____

_____

_____

3. Lakes are among our most valuable natural resources. Jot down their value to us in the space provided.

_____

_____

_____

4. Many of our lakes are in danger of dying. How has man caused the death of many lakes?

_____

_____

_____

GA1309

RING OF FIRE

There is a zone called the *Ring of Fire* that surrounds the land areas that ring the Pacific Ocean where the plates that support the land areas meet the plates that cradle the ocean. Where this occurs, the edges of the plates of the ocean slide under the plates that support the continents. They bend downward into the mantle within the earth which is very hot. When the plates grind together, the heat that results combines with the heat from within the earth to form a thick liquid called *magma*.

As the magma becomes hotter, it expands and builds up pressure in the surrounding area. It is also lighter than the surrounding rock, causing it to rise through the overlying plates. It rushes to the surface where it explodes out the top of the volcano as *lava*.

The map below shows the area called the Ring of Fire. Many of the earth's active volcanoes are found within this area. Among them are those in the list below. Find out the location of each and pinpoint that location on the outline map.

Mt. Fuji	Mt. St. Helens	Mayon
Mt. Katmai	Mauna Loa	El Chichón
Augustine	Kilauea	Paricutin

ECLIPSES

Planets and their satellites constantly in orbit around the sun sometimes reach positions respective to each other, when one body casts its own shadow on another. When this happens the phenomena is called an *eclipse*. While the moon revolves around the earth, both the earth and the moon revolve around the sun. There are occasions when the earth lies perfectly in a line between the sun and the moon. During those occasions the moon moves through the earth's shadow causing the moon to be blocked out from the sun's light. This phenomena is called a *lunar eclipse* (see diagram to the right).

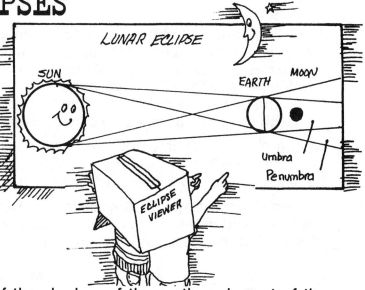

When the moon enters first into the path of the shadow of the earth, only part of the sun's light is blocked out, so we can still see the moon, but it appears gray in color. This shadow stage is referred to as the *penumbra*. As time passes, the deep shadow of the earth covers the entire face of the moon in a stage called the *umbra*. During such times, the moon is only dimly lit. There is still enough light that bends around the earth to allow us to see the moon. Its color, however, appears to be a coppery red.

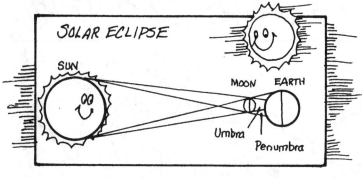

Between two and five times each year, the sun and earth line up in a position where the moon lies between the two. When this happens, the moon's shadow falls on the earth, blocking out much of the sun's light cast toward earth. When this happens, the event is called a *solar eclipse* (see diagram to left). Such occasions are rare to view by people on earth because the total eclipse is seen only where the moon's deep shadow falls. The moon is much smaller than the earth so the chances of viewing a total solar eclipse are small unless the viewer is in the right place on earth. More people lie in the areas outside in the view of the partial shadow (penumbra), but many people on earth experience no shadows at all because they lie outside the viewing area.

1. When the moon lies between the sun and the earth, causing the moon to cast a shadow on earth, which type of eclipse is taking place? _____

2. When the earth lies between the sun and the moon, causing the earth to cast its shadow on the moon, which type of eclipse is taking place? _____

3. Which is more commonly viewed by people on earth, a solar eclipse or a lunar eclipse? _____

4. What is the term used to describe a deep shadow? _____

5. What term is used to describe a partial shadow? _____

6. There are some occasions when the moon's umbra doesn't even reach the earth. How do you explain? _____

7. Can you think of reasons why people in ancient times were terrified of eclipses?

_____

GA1309

GRASSLANDS

Those areas on earth that are dominated by grass as the natural vegetation are called *grasslands*. The amount of annual rainfall plays a large role in the type of vegetation found in a given area. Grasslands occur in areas that get more rainfall than a desert (less than ten inches per year) and less rainfall than forests (which receive over thirty inches per year).

There are two main varieties of grasslands—*temperate grasslands* and *tropical grasslands*. Temperate grasslands are found where there are definite temperature and seasonal variations. Tropical grasslands are located in regions near the equator where it is hot the year around. The only differences in their seasons is the amount of rain that falls during the rainy and dry times of year. The major use of grasslands is agricultural purposes with almost three fourths of the world's food being grown on rich and fertile grassland soils.

GA1309

GRASSLANDS

Below is a map of the earth's major grasslands. Depending on the locations of these lands, the names used to describe them vary from one place to another. Identify the location of each of the following by labeling its location on the outline map: steppe, pampas, veld, prairie, savannahs, Serengeti Plain.

Where the Grasslands Are Found

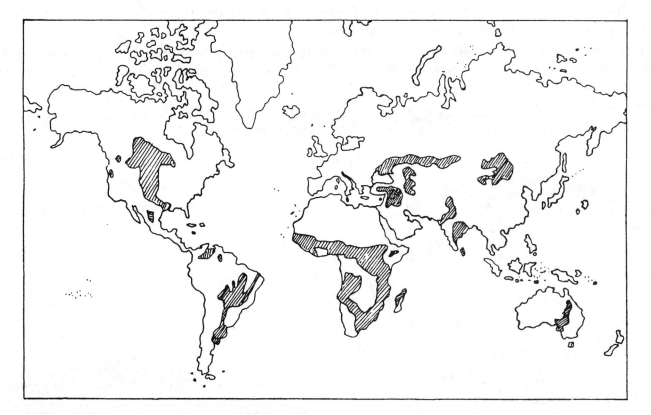

1. There are millions of insects living in grassland areas. There are also many birds and burrowing animals like the prairie dog and the suslik. Find out what benefit burrowing animals are to grasslands.

_____

_____

_____

2. One of the dangers to our grasslands is their being overgrazed. First, what is causing the overgrazing? Respond also to the extent of the damage done to the land when overgrazing occurs.

_____

_____

_____

3. Our natural grasslands are fast disappearing not only because of overgrazing but also because of urban development and overcultivation. The Dust Bowl of the 1930's in the United States is a good example of what happens to grasslands when they are overcultivated. If we are to save our grasslands for future generations, what are some courses of action we should be taking now?

_____

_____

_____

62

ECOSYSTEMS

An *ecosystem* includes all of the living and nonliving things that are found within a given community. The interaction of these living things as well as their action on the nonliving things combine to make it a system of depending that works and sustains all that lives within. If an element is removed from the system, problems develop, and the entire system can be thrown out of sync. There are often smaller ecosystems that live within the structure of the large ecosystem.

Biomes are the largest ecosystems into which the earth's land surface can be divided. Each is named after the vegetation that is found there. Each is also the home of a wide variety of plants and animals.

Below is a map of the earth's major ecosystems. Your task is to match the letter you find on the map to the word that is used to describe the ecosystem.

1. _I_ MOUNTAIN
2. _J_ MAQUIS
3. _F_ SAVANNAH
4. _G_ DESERT

5. _A_ TROPICAL FOREST
6. _C_ DECIDUOUS FOREST
7. _H_ ICE

8. _B_ CONIFEROUS FOREST
9. _D_ TUNDRA
10. _E_ TEMPERATE GRASSLAND

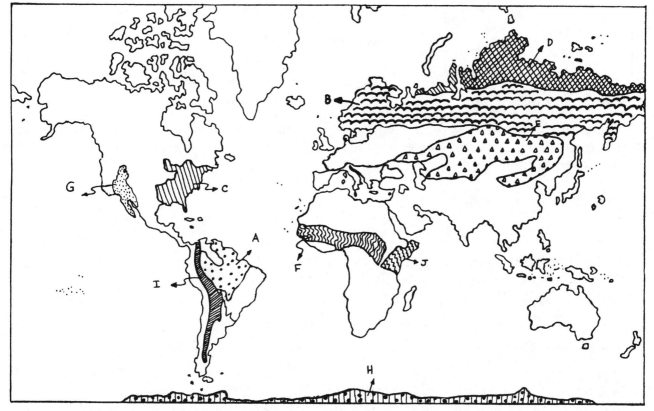

Create your own key in the space below.

MAPPING AN ECOSYSTEM

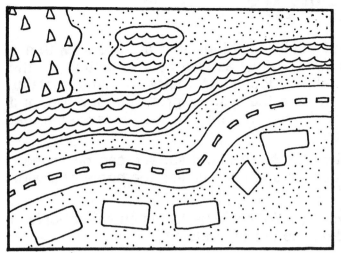

There are several ecosystems that are an ongoing day-to-day part of the environment in which you live. To become more familiar with what they are and what they mean to you, first obtain a local map of the area where you live. Next, using this map, go out and explore a small area of that map. Take a notebook along to record what you see. Then, in the space below, draw a map of your own of the area which you investigated. Label the important areas you visited and the locations of all the ecosystems you were able to find and identify.

GA1309

EROSION

For millions of years the forces of nature have been shaping and reshaping the face of the earth and its environments. Wind, ice, water and gravity are the chief agents involved in this changing process. As they move, they cause physical changes to the face of the earth. Some of these changes are rapid, while others take millions of years. Even the slow changes often result in dramatic changes to the earth. Moving glaciers cause deep valleys; snow and heavy rains can cause avalanches. The force of gravity is constantly at work moving material that may be on a slope or hillside. The wind can sculpture sand and rocks and the combined forces of wind, water and ice can create deltas and dunes.

Changes are also made to the earth by man. Farming, urban and industrial development have all played a role in some rather dramatic changes to the earth's surface in a short period of time. Sometimes these changes have not been good for the land.

1. In the space below describe some observations you have made on your own where the forces of nature were responsible for erosion.

_____
_____
_____
_____
_____

2. We usually think of the term *erosion* in a negative way because of the destruction it sometimes causes. There are, however, some positive effects of erosion. Can you think of any?

_____
_____
_____
_____
_____

3. What are some techniques currently in use to prevent erosion to our land?

_____
_____
_____
_____
_____

GA1309

RICHTER SCALE

The *Richter scale* is a method developed by Charles F. Richter for measuring the intensity of earthquakes. The scale relies on a *seismograph* to measure the waves of vibration caused by the release of energy during an earthquake. The magnitude of these vibrations is expressed with a number. Seismologists can compare the intensity of earthquakes and the damage they cause by their numeric positions on the Richter scale.

A difference of one unit on the scale represents a magnitude of about 30 times the amount of energy released. For example, an earthquake that is recorded as a 5 on the Richter scale has a magnitude of approximately 30 times greater than an earthquake that is recorded as a 4. One that is recorded as a 6 would release about 900 times more energy than the earthquake that was a 4 on the Richter scale. While there is no measure in units of energy released, the Richter scale does give seismologists a handle for comparing one earthquake with another.

They know that a 2 can barely be felt and that a 5 or greater can cause damage to property. Any earthquake that is recorded with a magnitude of 8 or more can be very destructive! A minus 2 is the smallest that seismologists can record. There are no limits to the other end of the scale, but those in the 8 and 9 range are the largest to date that have been recorded. Quakes are often reported in tenths of a whole unit (for example, a 6.5) to give the public more accurate levels of magnitude of various earthquakes.

1. How much greater would an earthquake with a magnitude of 6 be on the Richter scale than one recorded as a 5? _____

2. How much greater would a quake recorded as a 7 be than an earthquake recorded as a 5? _____

3. How much greater would an 8 be than an earthquake recorded as a 5 on the scale?

   _____

4. Earthquakes are recorded in tenths of a unit on the Richter scale. How much greater would the magnitude of a quake recorded as a 7.5 be than one recorded as a 5?

   _____

5. What are the benefits and values of the Richter scale?

   _____

   _____

   _____

   _____

   _____

   _____

   _____

   _____

GREENHOUSE EFFECT

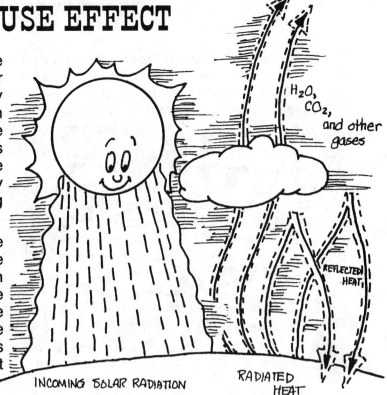

The carbon dioxide that is found in the atmosphere is important to keeping our earth warm. This is accomplished by trapping the sun's heat in a phenomenon known as the *greenhouse effect*. The atmosphere allows sunlight to easily pass through the earth's surface. However, the carbon dioxide then traps the heat by preventing the radiation from escaping back into space.

The sunlight passes freely through the atmosphere on its way to the earth where it is absorbed by the ground. The earth then radiates heat back toward the atmosphere as infrared radiation. Carbon dioxide absorbs this infrared radiation, causing the gases to warm. Some of the heated gas escapes back into the atmosphere, but much of it is directed back to earth.

Without this warming phenomena, the earth would be very cold. However, the burning of fossil fuels on our industrialized earth has greatly increased the amount of carbon dioxide and methane in the atmosphere. The result is these gases absorbing greater amounts of infrared radiation and thus more heat. As the effect becomes stronger, it is reasonable to expect that the earth will become warmer.

Some scientists predict that the greenhouse effect will result in the earth warming by as much as 5^0-10^0 F within the next century. Think of the long-term effects of this warming and describe what you feel could be the implications of such a changed world in the space below.

GA1309

PLATEAUS

Along with mountains, plains and hills, *plateaus* are one of earth's four major landforms. They are defined as flat lands that stand above the surrounding area. They occur when the earth's crust is uplifted by the interaction of its plates from within. The shifting and colliding of these plates over a period of time causes sections of the crust to rise.

Often a cross-sectional view of a plateau will reveal alternative horizontal layers of hard and soft rock. Erosion and the forces of nature will eventually wear down the plateau until it reaches a layer of hard rock called *caprock* that is resistant to further erosion. Plateaus also are characterized by steep sides which develop when rivers form deep valleys by cutting through the caprock. When a plateau is broken up by weather and erosion, the smaller sections are called *outliers*.

If the area is wider than it is high, it is called a *mesa*. Smaller outliers which are separated from mesas and have smaller caps and eventually can become slender spires of rock are called *buttes*. Plateaus, mesas and buttes are found all over the world. In the United States, this geological phenomena is quite pronounced in the Southwest. If the area is dry, as it is there, the landforms tend to keep their same basic shapes. In wetter areas, erosion tends to round the edges of these high flat tablelands.

Look at the drawing at the top of this page and label the various landforms presented above. Include the terms: plateau, mesa, butte. Show your knowledge of the definitions of these terms by discussing them in a paragraph below written in your own words.

_____

_____

_____

_____

_____

_____

_____

MOUNTAINS

Geologists define *mountains* as landforms that are more than 1000 feet (300 m) higher than the land nearby. Mountains are found on every continent as one of the earth's four major landforms. They are also found in many areas of the ocean floor. In fact the earth's largest mountain chain (Mid-Ocean Ridge) is mostly hidden beneath the sea.

Mountains are created in one of the following four ways:

Fold mountains are the result of the interaction of the earth's plates. As the plates collide, the crust of the earth is folded and the resultant wrinkle pushed upward. Some of the earth's tallest mountains were formed in this manner.

Volcano mountains are created when molten rock explodes from within the earth. As the volcanoes erupt, the lava and ash cooks and forms a cone that continues to build as other eruptions occur. Volcanic mountains are formed under the ocean as well as on land.

Dome mountains develop when molten rock forms create large buildup within the earth's crust, causing the surface to bulge. The magma then slowly hardens into igneous rock creating a domed formation.

Fault-block mountains are created when movement takes place along a fault or break in the earth's crust. The rock on one side of the fault rises higher than the rock on the other side creating a steep wall on one side and a more gentle side on the other.

GA1309

MOUNTAINS

1. Below are examples of mountains that were formed in each of the four ways. Your task is to find out about each and match by letter.

_____ Black Hills   a. fold mountain

_____ Mount Fuji   b. dome mountain

_____ Sierra Nevada   c. volcanic mountain

_____ Himalayas   d. fault-block mountain

2. As one climbs up the side of a mountain, the climber is actually getting closer to the sun. In that sense, it would seem like it should get warmer as the climber goes higher. We all know, however, this is not the case. Why does it get colder as one climbs higher and higher on a mountain?

_____

_____

_____

_____

3. Because we know there is a direct relationship between elevation and temperature, we know that those mountains that are very tall have a wide variety of vegetation and climate environments. The higher we go, the colder it gets. These various environments are called *life zones*. Below is a drawing containing various plant and animal life. The vegetation is determined by the temperature and the length of the growing season. Label each and describe the kind of plant and animal life found there: deciduous trees, coniferous trees, pastures, alpine meadows, permanent snow.

4. On the map that follows are shown the world's most important mountain systems. Find each on the map and label its proper location.

Andes
Rocky Mountains
Appalachians
Guiana Highlands
Pyrenees
Sierra Madre
Occidental
Kunlun Mountains

Atlas Mountain
Alps
Carpathian Mountains
Cascades
Sierra Nevada
Zagros Mountains
Drakensberg
Greater Khingan Range

Great Dividing Range
Himalayas
Ural Mountains
Coastal Mountains
Altai Mountains
Tian Shan
Hindu Kush
Ethiopian Highlands

GA1309

THE WORLD'S MOUNTAIN SYSTEMS

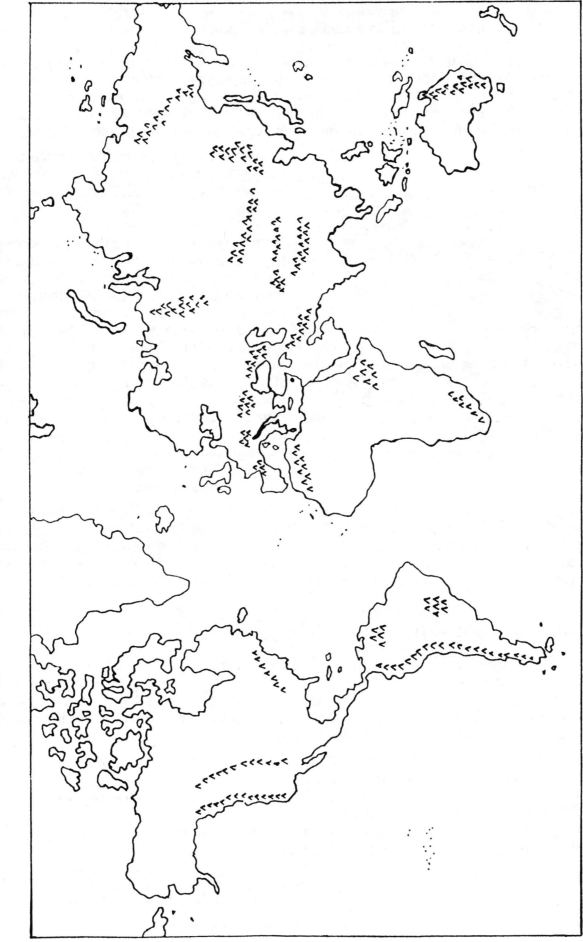

71

GA1309

HURRICANES

A *hurricane* is a tropical storm with wind speeds of at least 74 miles (119 km) per hour. These storms are also known as *cyclones* and *typhoons* in other parts of the world, but all three terms describe the same type of tropical storm. Hurricanes develop most often during the summer and fall when water temperatures are the warmest. Winds from the Northern and Southern Hemispheres come together causing tropical disturbances.

Under certain conditions these disturbances can grow into tropical depressions which include a low pressure center and heavy thunderstorms. As the depressions travel over the warm ocean, they draw energy from the warm water. As they gain strength, these depressions gather large amounts of moisture. The low pressure center gains strength and the winds get stronger and the result is a tropical storm. A tropical depression becomes a tropical storm when the winds reach 39 miles (63 km) per hour. Some tropical storms gain hurricane strength as they move across the ocean and eventually head for land. As the hurricanes hit the land, the high winds can cause severe damage, but the greatest damage is done by the water that slams into the land in the form of huge waves and torrential downpours.

1. During each hurricane season, the Weather Service creates a list of names that will be used to identify tropical storms. The names are the first names of people. Each year the new list begins with a name that starts with the letter A and continues alphabetically. The list is alternated each year between names for men and names for women. Identify the names included in this year's list in the space below.

_____

_____

_____

_____

2. Hurricanes are also known as cyclones and typhoons. The three terms are used synonomously. It's merely a case of location. Identify the name used for these tropical storms in each of the following locations:

   Atlantic Ocean or Eastern Pacific _____

   Northern Indian Ocean and Bay of Bengal _____

   West Pacific _____

3. How have the casualties and loss of life been reduced in recent years by the methods employed by the National Hurricane Center?

_____

_____

_____

_____

GA1309

OCEANS

The oceans form the earth's largest ecosystem covering over 70 percent of the surface of the planet. Even though it is one continuous expanse of water that surrounds the continents, geographers have assigned different names to its various parts. The four largest of those parts are known as the Atlantic, Pacific, Indian and Arctic Oceans. Without the oceans, life on earth would not be possible.

The underwater landscape of the ocean is just as varied in structure and appearance as that on land. There are huge mountains, deep canyons and vast plains. Our oceans are filled with thousands of different communities and habitats. Because of its huge surface area, huge quantities of water evaporate into the atmosphere where they condense into clouds and fall as rain. This cycle is very important to life on earth.

The sun warms the ocean waters. The heat from the water then warms the atmosphere which helps to keep the earth warm and livable. Without this heat the earth would be very cold.

Food Webs

The ocean is a vast food web. Below are listed the elements of one such web. Arrange them in the order of their dependency and draw arrows to show the relationship.

blue whale, tuna, zooplankton, herring, phytoplankton

73

GA1309

OCEANS

Using the attached map, label the various physical features of the ocean landscape listed below.

Atlantic Ocean
Pacific Ocean
Indian Ocean
Arctic Ocean
East Siberian Sea
North Sea
Coral Sea
Baltic Sea
Arabian Sea
Mediterranean Sea
Bay of Bengal
South China Sea
Gulf of Mexico

Mid-Atlantic Ridge
Pacific Antarctic Ridge
East Pacific Ridge
Weddell Abyssal Plain
Mid-Indian Ocean Ridge
Ninetyeast Ridge
Wilkes Abyssal Plain
Aleutian Trench
Clarion Fracture Zone
Great Australian Bight
Carlesberg Ridge
Kuril Trench
Mid-Ocean Canyon

Deep-Sea Projects

- While the ocean provides us with food and many other resources, there are current threats to their future. Overfishing has been responsible for the disappearance of some species and has been the cause of others to be dangerously threatened with extinction. Oil spills, pesticides and factory wastes also pose dangers to the life of our oceans. Research these topics in terms of the current situation and create a list of the most current problems and what is being done to solve them.

- In addition to the wealth of food that comes from the oceans, there are many valuable resources. Find out about some of these other resources and present a listing below of those you consider of greatest value.

_____

_____

_____

_____

- Find out about the current techniques that are in use to measure the depth of the ocean. Explain how the concept of sonar works.

_____

_____

_____

_____

_____

_____

GA1309

LANDFORMS IN THE OCEAN

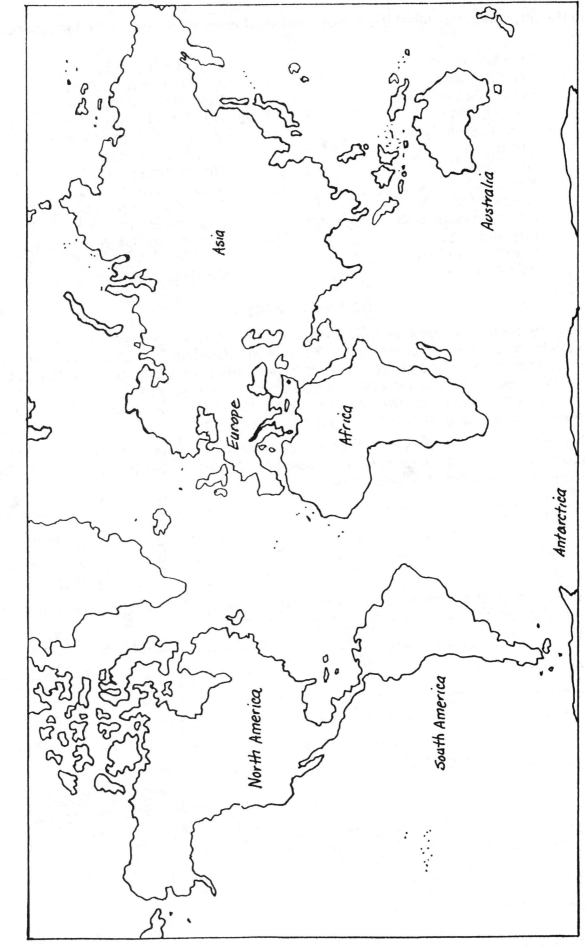

GA1309

OCEAN CURRENTS

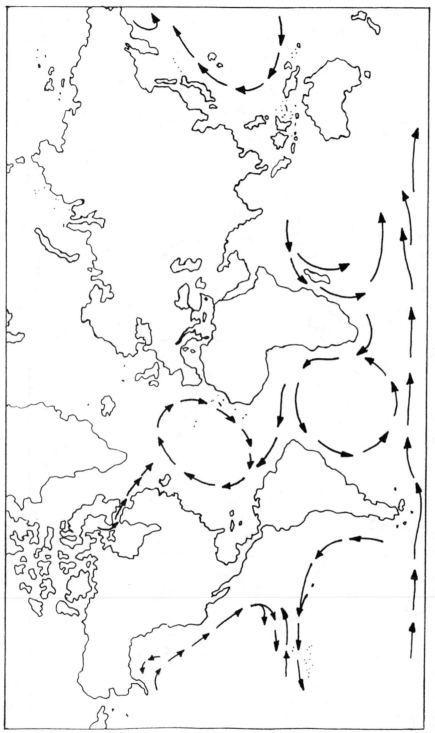

Above is an outline map of the world with arrows showing the general paths of the most important ocean currents.

a. California Current
b. North Equatorial Current
c. South Equatorial Current
d. Equatorial Counter Current
e. Peru Current
f. Gulf Stream

g. Brazilian Current
h. West Wind Drift
i. Benguela Current
j. Agulhas Current
k. Labrador Current

Refer back to the map and identify each of the ocean currents by the letter that corresponds to each current listed above. Then circle with a blue pen those currents that are cold water currents, and use a red pen to circle the warm water currents.

GA1309

DEEP-SEA DATA

Below are some questions about our oceans which have no doubt caused you to be curious before. With your "in-depth" study of the oceans, you probably now know the answers. If not, find out and record your answers in the spaces below.

1. Why are there currents in the ocean?

_____

_____

_____

_____

2. Why is the water in the ocean salty?

_____

_____

_____

_____

3. What causes waves to break as they approach the shore?

_____

_____

_____

_____

4. Why do the tides rise and fall?

_____

_____

_____

_____

5. Why are there ripple marks in the sand on beaches?

_____

_____

_____

_____

GA1309

DESERTS

Deserts are those areas on earth which receive less than ten inches (25.4 cm) of precipitation annually. Deserts are found on every continent and cover roughly one third of the earth's land surface. They are home to almost one billion people. Some are mountainous and some are flat; some are hot and some are cold. The common ground is always the lack of rainfall. The reasons for the lack of rain, however, vary and are the basis for the five different kinds of deserts that exist. The map below shows the locations of the major deserts on earth.

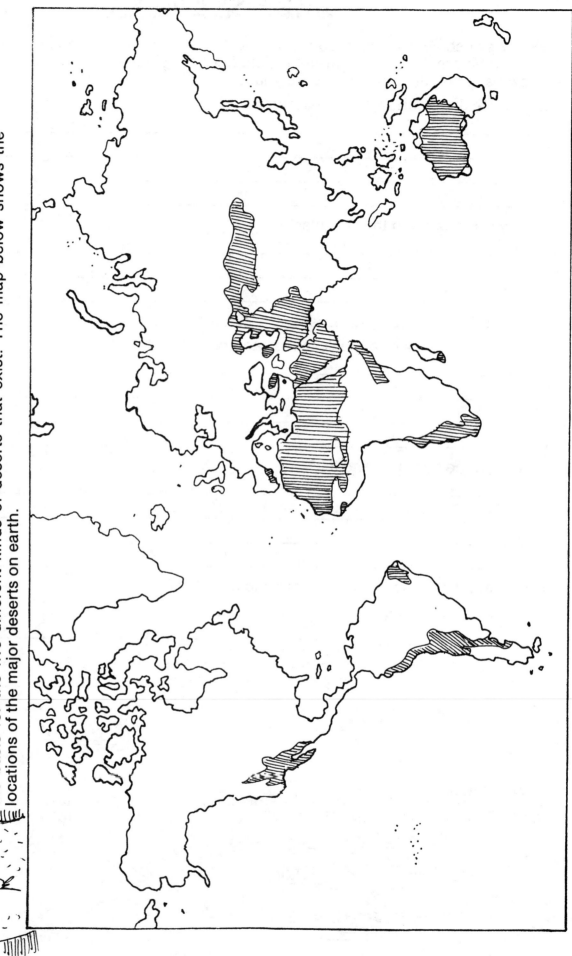

GA1309

KINDS OF DESERTS

1. Most of the earth's dry lands are found in a belt near the tropic of Cancer, north of the equator or another belt near the tropic of Capricorn, south of the equator. Those desert regions are known as *subtropical deserts*. Earth's largest desert, the Great Sahara, is a subtropical desert. Find out the explanation for subtropical deserts lacking rainfall and jot down your answer in the space below.

   _____

   _____

   _____

   _____

2. Cold ocean currents that invade the shorelines of land masses are the cause for *coastal deserts*. Find out the scientific explanation for such areas being very dry. The Atacama Desert in Chile is an example of a coastal desert.

   _____

   _____

   _____

   _____

3. *Interior deserts* are found in the interior of large land masses. The Gobi Desert in Asia is an example of an interior desert. Research and record your explanation for the cause of interior deserts in the space below.

   _____

   _____

   _____

   _____

GA1309

KINDS OF DESERTS

4. *Polar deserts* are found in Antarctica and in some regions of the Arctic. Again, the criterion for their definition as desert areas comes from their lack of rainfall. In fact, it isn't a lack of moisture that causes these regions to be so dry. Perhaps you can guess the answer to this one. Jot down your explanation for polar deserts in the space below.

_____

_____

_____

5. *Rain shadow deserts* are found in areas near mountains. The desert conditions are always on the side of the mountain range that faces away from the wind. Patagonia in Argentina is an example of a rain shadow desert. Find out the cause for this kind of desert and jot your answer in the space below.

_____

_____

_____

6. On your outline map, showing where the world's major deserts are located, pinpoint the location of each of the following:

Atacama   Antarctica   Gobi
Patagonia   Australian outback   Kalahari
Great Sahara

Desertification is the process by which marginal grasslands are transformed into useless deserts. Any number of factors can be the blame when this happens. Find out about the culprits and list all the possible reasons in the space below.

_____

_____

_____

_____

GA1309

LIFE IN THE DESERT

The secret to surviving in the desert lies in *adaptation. Adaptation* means "a long-term interaction with the environment resulting in either physical change or behaviorial change and in some cases both." Just as the Aborigines who first inhabited the Australian outback made changes in their life-style, so have plants and animals made changes necessary to survive under the harsh conditions of the desert. Take note of the examples below.

The marsupial mouse has become a nocturnal animal, staying in a burrow during the heat of the day and then searching for food at night. The animal also stores fat in its tail for use during times of food shortage.

Cacti have spines rather than leaves, the result being less water loss through evaporation.

The North American jackrabbit has developed large ears that help to radiate away the body's heat.

The camel is another animal which stores fat for later use. The hump does not contain water, but fat that is changed into water as needed by combining hydrogen within the fat with oxygen inhaled by the camel.

These are but a few of the adaptations that have taken place among the living species that survive on deserts. In the space below, cite two other examples. Explain each adaptation and then share your findings with other members of the class.

_____
_____
_____
_____
_____
_____
_____
_____

GA1309

ADAPTING FOR COMFORT

Those who live in the desert are aware that the environment is one of drastic contrasts. Scorching temperatures of the noonday sun are replaced by nights with the thermometer often dipping into the 40's or lower. While it seldom rains in the desert, torrential downpours are commonplace when it does rain, with several inches falling sometimes in a single hour. With little vegetation to stop them, strong desert winds can add further to the discomfort.

With almost one billion people living in deserts, they have made a number of adjustments to make their lives more livable and comfortable. Read from other sources about how people live in the desert and record a summary of your findings for each of the following. Then share your statements with other members of your class.

Homes _____

_____

_____

_____

Clothing _____

_____

_____

_____

Food _____

_____

_____

_____

Work _____

_____

_____

_____

Quality of Life _____

_____

_____

_____

The desert Southwest in the United States is experiencing a population explosion that is definitely weather-related. What are the reasons for people choosing to live in a desert climate? How does their life-style compare to the lives of those you researched earlier? Would you like living in a desert? What are the advantages and disadvantages? Discuss your thoughts on the back of this page.

GA1309

FORESTS

Forests are large areas where the trees are close enough together to shade the ground and thus prevent the growth of vegetation that would normally be found there. There are three major types of forests on the earth. They are tropical rain forests, coniferous forests and deciduous forests. Each is different in composition from the other two, but there are areas where the climate is right for forests to be mixed. Looking at the map below, you will see that forests are found on all continents of the earth except one. Which continent has no forests? Look at the map once again. What percentage of the earth's surface would you estimate is covered by forests?

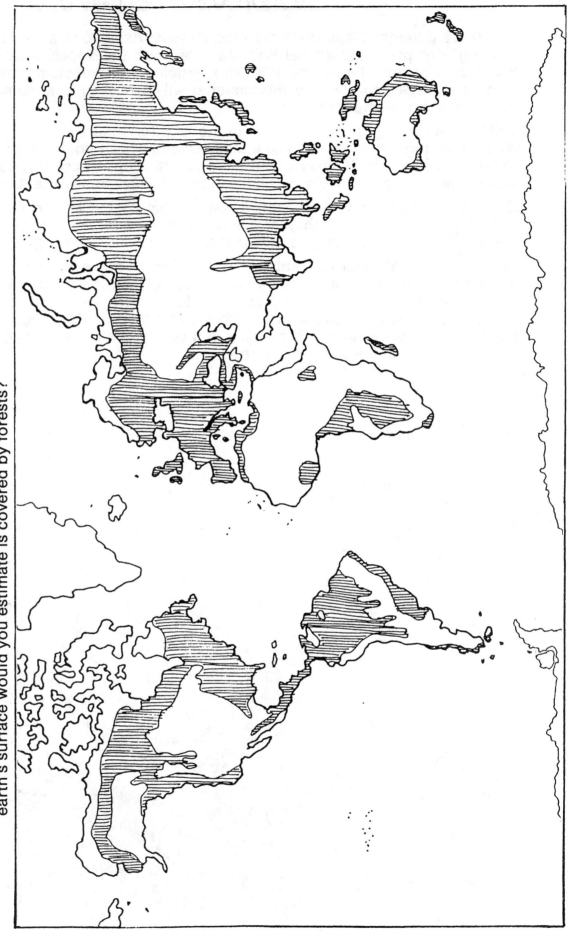

KINDS OF FORESTS

The three different kinds of forests—coniferous, deciduous and tropical rain—are all teeming with plant and animal life. That life gives the appearance of each a distinct look that separates it from the other two. Tropical rain forests are the topic of another study area (see page 54), so this material will deal with comparing and contrasting coniferous and deciduous forests.

Coniferous forests get their name from the fact that their seeds are produced in cones. Most of the trees growing in these forests have needles rather than leaves. It is common to find these forests in areas where there is not a lot of rainfall. The needles lose less water to evaporation than leaves, so these trees survive under drier conditions.

Deciduous forests derive their name by the meaning of the word *deciduous* which means "losing its leaves once each year." Most deciduous forests are found in areas where the temperature is mild and the rainfall is abundant.

Below is a list of plant and animal life that are at home in forests. Some are found in coniferous forests; some are more commonly seen in deciduous forests. Your task is to decide which one is a more appropriate answer. Decide not by merely guessing, but by researching the two kinds of forests and then making your decision. Place the letter *C* in the blank spaces beside life in a coniferous forest and the letter *D* in those that correspond to the deciduous forests.

1. _____ firs
2. _____ oak
3. _____ woodpecker
4. _____ ash
5. _____ grey squirrel
6. _____ Canadian goose
7. _____ pine
8. _____ maple
9. _____ bear

10. _____ moose
11. _____ birch
12. _____ butterfly
13. _____ chipmunk
14. _____ spruce
15. _____ larch
16. _____ yellow warbler
17. _____ wolf
18. _____ cedar

GA1309

HIDING IN THE FOREST

Hidden in the forest of letters below are twenty-seven words that are associated with forests. Your task is to find them. Some are horizontal, some are vertical and some are in reverse. Find each word in the list and circle.

deciduous
coniferous
evergreen
tropical rain forest
canopy
maple
birch
turpentine
gums

broadleaf
needle
spruce
boreal
taiga
fir
oak
resin
ash

rubber
understory
mosses
ferns
shrubs
forest floor
wildflowers
vines
pine

```
A T R U B U N A T W E T O H O S A M I W
T S E R O F N I A R L A C I P O R T W I
P H S A R I F N I Y R O T S R E D N U L
A I I E E O E E G C F S T O P S S A N D
S N N O A B S E A R O O L F T S E R O F
Y M A P L E A D B E L O H K N R N T T L
V E Y I F A E L D A O R B H C M I E D O
L N S N O Y N E E R G R E V E O V T N W
M I O L S P R U C E D S B U R H S W O E
E T G N N O A K I T H A I H E T H P S R
Z N T E R N H E D N C A N H E R R L I S
Q E S R E A A C U D R T F A F E F E F O
U P E S F C I C O N I F E R O U S V E R
Y R U B B E R T U H B O R G H O E D S I
P U E M O S S E S V U T N N I E N I P O
K T E M O B S E U T T T S M U G N K O G
```

GA1309

LEAFY PROJECTS

Tree in a Pot

There is an absolutely wonderful feeling associated with growing a tree that you yourself start with a mere seed. To do this, you'll have to wait until the seeds have fallen off the trees. Simply plant the seeds in small pots that are filled with a moist compost. When the seeds germinate in the spring, they will be ready for planting. When the young tree is about 6-8 inches (20 cm) tall, it is ready for the ground. Dig a hole the size of the pot and then remove the sapling and compost from that pot. Place in the ground, water the tree regularly and place a protection fence around the whole area.

Plant a Tree

First be certain to choose a kind of tree that will grow well in your area. Dig a hole that is deep enough to allow the tree to sit in a position where the root and the stem meet (called the collar). Drive a stake into the ground next to the tree to be used for support. Soak the root system before planting the tree. Place soil in the hole and shake the sapling to get soil between the roots. Firmly tap the soil and add more until the hole is filled. Support the tree's straight growth by tying the sapling to the stake with a rubber tie. Water the tree regularly and place mulch around it to prevent weeds from growing.

How Tall That Tree

Take a friend along to help you estimate the height of several trees using the following technique. Stand in front of the tree and have your friend back away from the tree holding a ruler at arm's length. When the top of your head reaches the mark of one inch on the ruler, your friend stops. Join your friend and together judge the level in inches that measures the top of the tree. Once that decision is made, simply multiply your own height in inches by the mark on the ruler. Divide the result by 12 to get the height of the tree in feet. For example, if your height is 4' 6" (54") and the top of the tree hits the 9-inch mark, the height of the tree is 486 inches or 40½ feet. Try this several times to improve your skill. Have another team measure the same tree and compare your results.

GA1309

MINERALS

There are over 2000 minerals that have been identified and classified by geologists according to their structure and composition. Each mineral contains a single chemical element or a combination of two or more. Minerals are very important to countries economically. Without them, a country has little chance of offering its people a promising standard of living through industrialization. Minerals are divided into metals and nonmetals. There are then subclassifications within each of these two major groups. The value of a mineral's worth is dependent upon its supply and demand. Those minerals which have a widespread use and are limited in supply bring a higher price in the market than those minerals which are abundant in quantity and have little use.

Below are the chemical symbols for some of the more widely used minerals. Identify the mineral and jot down some of the uses that are made of each.

Chemical Symbol	Mineral	Uses
Au		
S		
Cu		
Fe		
C		
U		
Ag		
Al		
NaCl		
N		
Hg		
SiO_2		

GA1309

READING A MINERAL MAP

Below is a map of the United States showing the locations where several important minerals are mined in the United States. Look carefully at the information contained on the map to answer the questions that follow. The numbers identify the top ten mineral states.

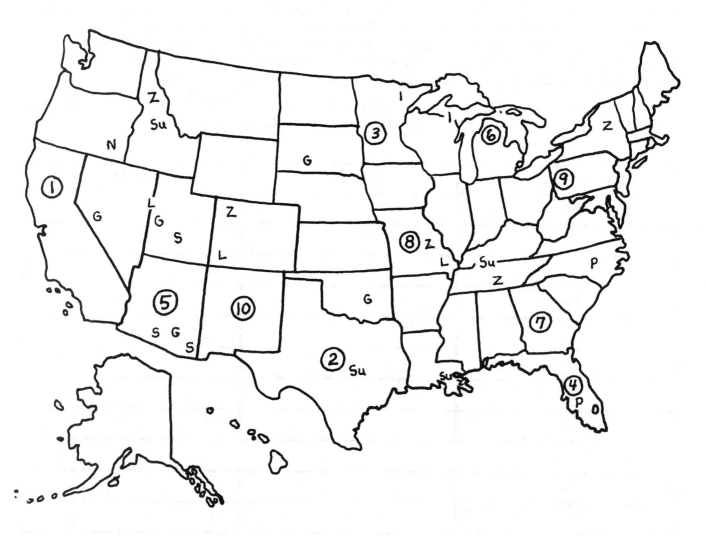

1. Which states have deposits of gold? _____

2. Name the states in which zinc is found? _____

3. Which states have deposits of silver? _____

4. In which states are there deposits of sulphur? _____

5. Which state leads the nation in the mining of all minerals? _____

6. Two states have significant deposits of phosphates. They are _____.

7. Which states have deposits of iron ore? _____

8. Which state ranks second in the mining of minerals in the United States? _____

9. Which two northern states rank high on the list in the mining of minerals? _____

10. Which states have major deposits of lead? _____

MINERAL DIG

Below is a list containing thirty words that are associated with the wealth of minerals found within our planet. Just as they are sometimes hard to find in the ground so may their names be difficult to find in the maze of letters below. Find each and circle the letters that spell the word.

mineral	tungsten	silver	silicate	uranium
iron	molybdenum	zinc	diamond	quartz
chromium	platinum	copper	phosphate rock	lead
cobalt	bauxite	tin	alloy	compound
manganese	mercury	aluminum	ferrous	halite
nickel	gold	graphite	sulphur	clay

```
P U S U L P H U R T E B D N U O P M O C
L M E R C U R Y T V T T O S U O R R E F
A O M A G L T R S R I W D I A M O N D O
T L A B O C O E N E H L M L L U S Y A G
I Y N A L H O V A P P I U I L I E M E S
N B G U D R F L S P A T N C O N T I L O
U D A X N O R I N O R I I A Y A I N A D
M E N I S M L S T C G T M T Y R L E I T
I N E T N I C K E L F I U E Q U A R T Z
W U S E T U N G S T E N L E B C H A E B
N M E W A M C N I Z D Y A L C I N L E N
T H I T E L I K C O R E T A H P S O H P
```

89

MAPS

A globe is more accurate in showing the true proportions and perspectives of places on earth than any flat wall map, regardless of its projection. That is because any rounded surface (which the earth is) must be distorted when shown on a flat surface. That is also why globes are essential tools when studying the geography of our world. But globes are difficult to carry around and they are also expensive. For these reasons, flat maps are much more useful and practical to those who study our earth.

There are, however, many different ways of graphically showing the earth. These various representations are called *projections*, and there are trade-offs in distortion for each kind of projection. Those who make maps are called *cartographers*. The task of the cartographer is to decide what to distort and what not to change as he makes his map. There is simply no way he can show everything the same way it is shown on a globe. The choices he makes will determine the kind of projections that result.

Below and on the next two pages are some of the kinds of projections that are most often used. Look closely at each and point out both the advantages and disadvantages of the projection. What is distorted and what is not?

EQUAL AREA MAP PROJECTION

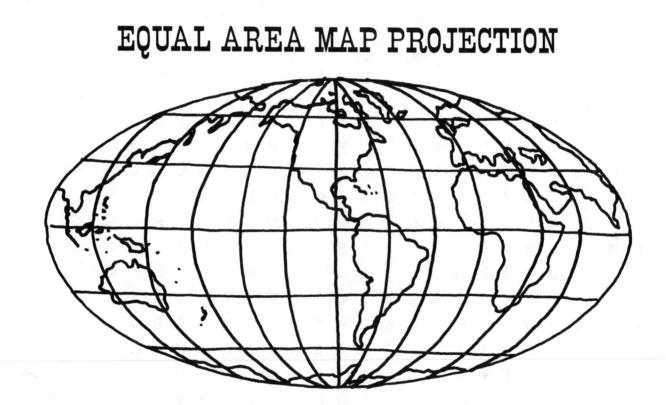

1. What is correct about the map above? _____

_____

2. What is distorted on this map of the world? _____

_____

　　　　　　　　　　　　　　　　　　　　　　　　　GA1309

MERCATOR'S CYLINDER PROJECTION

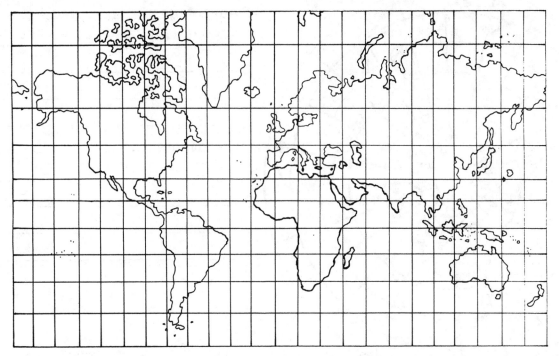

1. The mercator projection map is very useful and popular as the classroom wall map. Its advantages as you see them: _____

_____

2. Disadvantages: _____

_____

CONIC

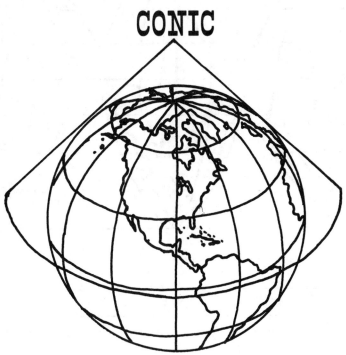

The conic projection is made from a perspective as if a cone were placed on a globe with its point directly above the North Pole.

3. Advantages: _____

4. Disadvantages: _____

91

POLAR PROJECTION

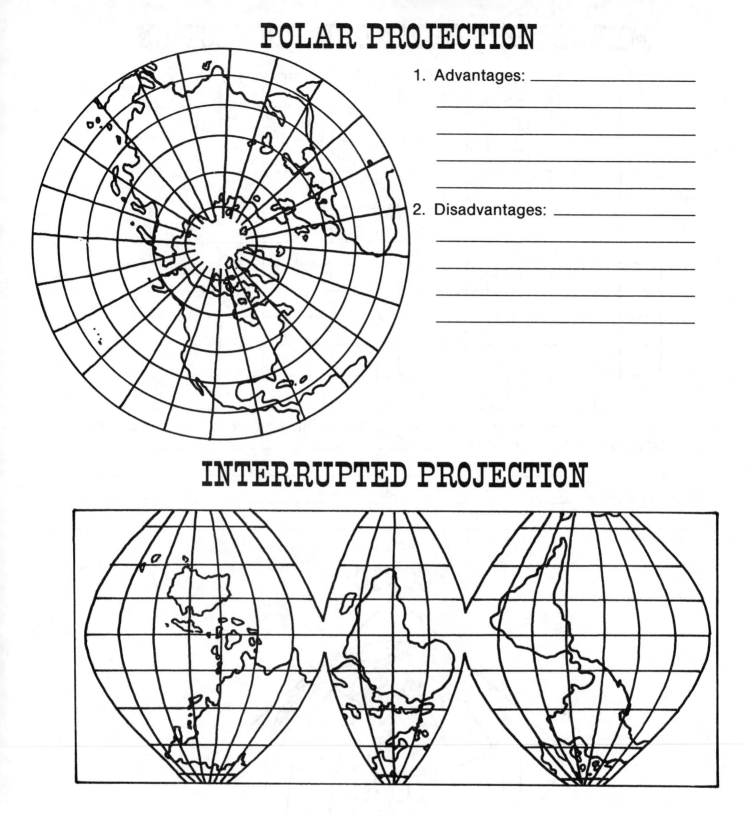

1. Advantages: _____
_____
_____
_____
_____

2. Disadvantages: _____
_____
_____
_____
_____
_____

INTERRUPTED PROJECTION

3. Advantages: _____

4. Disadvantages: _____

GA1309

HIDDEN MAP WORDS

Below are hidden thirty words that have something to do with maps. Circle the letters that correctly spell each word you find. Some are horizontal; some are vertical; some even appear in reverse.

projection	mountains	cartographer	key	region
mercator	population	rivers	states	continents
polar	conic	globe	climate	graphic
hills	landforms	plains	boundaries	road
lakes	plateaus	oceans	elevation	resources
physical	lowlands	scale	map	symbols

```
G Y I R E H P A R G O T R A C
R T W S E C R U O S E R S C O
A B D M A P E L E V A T I O N
P O S M R O F D N A L I R H T
H U C L G L O B E U H K E I I
I N O I T A L U P O P A G I N
C D N M E R C A T O R O I V E
K A I S N I A T N U O M O I N
L R C L S N A E C O J C N S T
A I P L A I N S S R E V I R S
C E T I D F O E L A C S O M N
I S A H A D S U A E T A L P I
S E H N O Y E K O R I R E O O
Y T N U R M K P S L O B M Y S
H A C L I M A T E S N E L U W
P T S D N A L W O L M D T O G
J S O S E T I T D O B E A E D
```

GA1309

MAJOR RIVERS

Rivers are essential to life on earth. Their fresh waters flow out into the seas and oceans where water evaporates, rises to form clouds, then condenses and falls as rain over the land. This water cycle and its supply of fresh water by rivers brings life to living things on the land. Rivers are found on virtually every major land mass. They have been important historically since before man began recording time. Many of the earth's major cities became major cities because of their locations near rivers. Their importance today is no less than it was thousands of years ago.

Rivers remain a major method of inexpensive transportation for shipping raw materials and bulk goods. They also provide hydroelectricity for millions of homes and factories. As the hand of man has tainted many of our natural resources, so has he fouled and polluted many of our rivers. Since the late 1960's, stricter laws and greater concern has brought many of our rivers back toward cleaner conditions, but much remains to be done. Environmentalists continue their battle to clean up and preserve our rivers, one of our greatest of natural resources.

Below are some of the world's great rivers. Match each river to the continent on which its waters flow.

Af = Africa, E = Europe, As = Asia, NA = North America, Au = Australia, SA = South America

1. _____ Thames	6. _____ St. Lawrence	11. _____ Murray
2. _____ Nile	7. _____ Yangtze	12. _____ Paraná
3. _____ Amazon	8. _____ Rhine	13. _____ Orinoco
4. _____ Mississippi	9. _____ Colorado	14. _____ Darling
5. _____ Volga	10. _____ Zaire	15. _____ Ganges

16. _____ Tiber	21. _____ Tigris
17. _____ Rhône	22. _____ Rio Grande
18. _____ Columbia	23. _____ Ob
19. _____ Niger	24. _____ Yellow
20. _____ Yukon	25. _____ Irrawaddy

GA1309

RIVERS OF THE WORLD

The major rivers of the world are drawn in on the map below. Locate each by matching the number to the correct name.

_____ Lena, _____ Niger, _____ Ganges, _____ Mackenzie, _____ Zaire, _____ Tennessee, _____ Missouri, _____ Yangtze, _____ Negro, _____ St. Lawrence, _____ Danube, _____ Amazon, _____ Volga, _____ Rio Grande, _____ Ob, _____ Mekong, _____ Rio de la Plata, _____ Indus, _____ Zambezi, _____ Thames, _____ Yukon, _____ Nile, _____ Mississippi, _____ Irtysh _____ Rhine, _____ Amur, _____ Colorado, _____ Brahmaputra, _____ Paraná, _____ Ohio, _____ Rhône, _____ Orinoco, _____ Yellow, _____ Darling

GA1309

GREAT RIVERS/GREAT CITIES

Many of the world's great cities have emerged as a result of being located on great rivers. Your task is to match the cities listed in the first column with the rivers on which they are located in the second column. The only twist is that the letters are all out of order. So you will have to unscramble the letters before you can match them up.

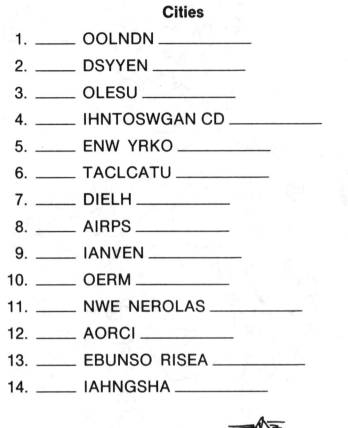

Cities	Rivers
1. _____ OOLNDN _____	a. YHOHGOL _____
2. _____ DSYYEN _____	b. CTMAOPO _____
3. _____ OLESU _____	c. INESE _____
4. _____ IHNTOSWGAN CD _____	d. HMTAES _____
5. _____ ENW YRKO _____	e. IBTRE _____
6. _____ TACLCATU _____	f. UODHSN _____
7. _____ DIELH _____	g. MARAPRTATA _____
8. _____ AIRPS _____	h. MANJU _____
9. _____ IANVEN _____	i. NHA _____
10. _____ OERM _____	j. UNDABE _____
11. _____ NWE NEROLAS _____	k. ELNI _____
12. _____ AORCI _____	l. SIISIMSSPIP _____
13. _____ EBUNSO RISEA _____	m. ALERDILAOPTA _____
14. _____ IAHNGSHA _____	n. ZNYTGAE _____

GA1309

ANATOMY OF A RIVER

Below are several terms that tell the story of a river. Your task is to become familiar with the terms, then to look carefully at the drawing below and pinpoint those areas of the map that illustrate the definitions of the words by matching the numbers to the words below.

____ source, ____ mouth, ____ delta, ____ tributary, ____ rapids, ____ marsh, ____ lake, ____ floodplain

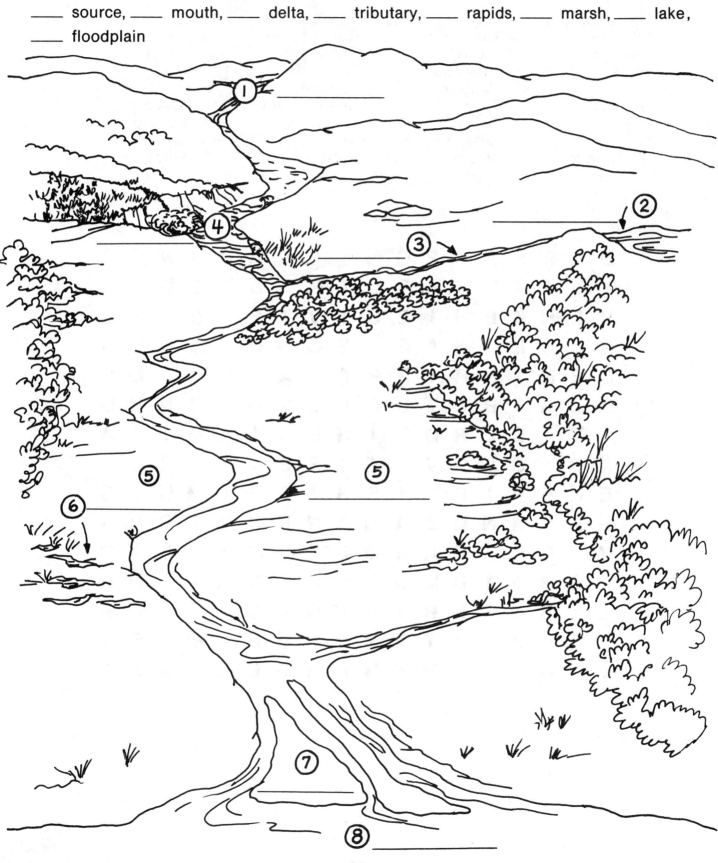

GA1309

HIDDEN RIVERS

Below are the letters that spell the names of thirty-six of the world's greatest rivers. Your task is to look at the list, find the letters in the scramble of letters and then circle those letters that spell the name of each river.

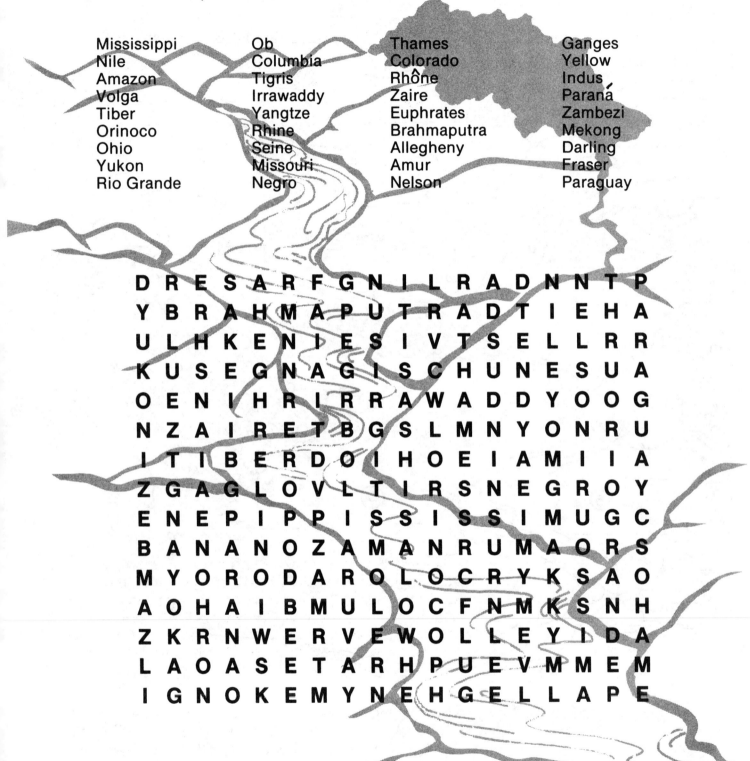

Mississippi	Ob	Thames	Ganges
Nile	Columbia	Colorado	Yellow
Amazon	Tigris	Rhône	Indus
Volga	Irrawaddy	Zaire	Paraná
Tiber	Yangtze	Euphrates	Zambezi
Orinoco	Rhine	Brahmaputra	Mekong
Ohio	Seine	Allegheny	Darling
Yukon	Missouri	Amur	Fraser
Rio Grande	Negro	Nelson	Paraguay

```
D R E S A R F G N I L R A D N N T P
Y B R A H M A P U T R A D T I E H A
U L H K E N I E S I V T S E L L R R
K U S E G N A G I S C H U N E S U A
O E N I H R I R R A W A D D Y O O G
N Z A I R E T B G S L M N Y O N R U
I T I B E R D O I H O E I A M I I A
Z G A G L O V L T I R S N E G R O Y
E N E P I P P I S S I S S I M U G C
B A N A N O Z A M A N R U M A O R S
M Y O R O D A R O L O C R Y K S A O
A O H A I B M U L O C F N M K S N H
Z K R N W E R V E W O L L E Y I D A
L A O A S E T A R H P U E V M M E M
I G N O K E M Y N E H G E L L A P E
```

CITIES

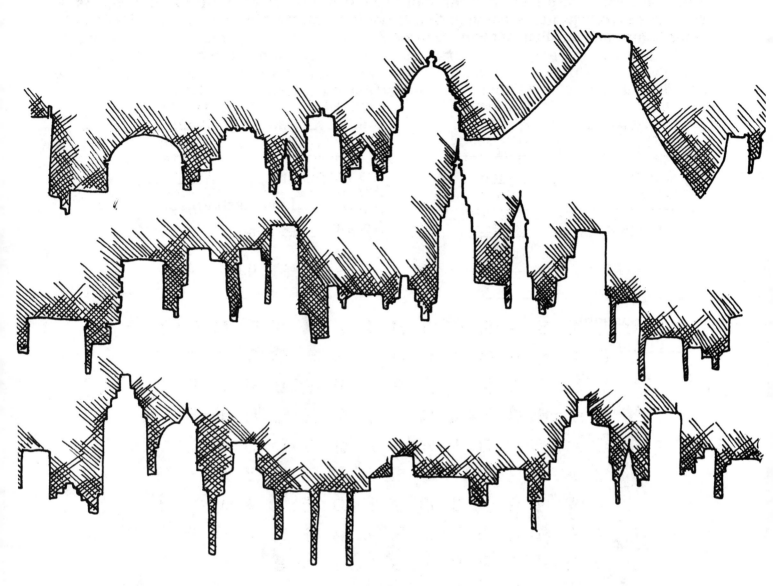

Three out of every four people in the United States live in metropolitan areas. By the turn of the century over half of the people who live in developed countries will live in cities. There is sometimes some confusion over the definition of what constitutes a city, with the deciding factor usually being a population count. For purposes of simplification, the use of the term in this material will refer to "any locality with a population of 2500 or more." Bear in mind, however, that in other parts of the world, the term carries a different meaning.

Cities have certain common characteristics, regardless of their locations. Houses are closer together, occupations are more specialized and the people themselves are more dependent upon each other than in rural areas. Cultural opportunities are more available as are job opportunities. The range of social classes is wider in cities and there are greater numbers of ethnic groups than in small towns and rural areas.

While life in the city is indeed exciting and moves at a fast pace, those who live there must contend with the higher crime rate, the health hazards, the high cost of living and the other problems that are a part of city living.

GA1309

THE WORLD'S LARGEST CITIES

Below are listed in groups of five, many of the world's largest cities. Your task is to rank order each group according to population. The only way you can do this is to consult an almanac that contains the most recent census figures. Place a #1 beside the largest city in each group, a #2 beside the second largest, etc., with a #5 beside the city in each group with the smallest population. In the blank to the right of the city, fill in the name of the country in which each city is located.

a. _____ Jakarta, _____

_____ Rio de Janeiro, _____

_____ Toronto, _____

_____ Copenhagen, _____

_____ Ahmadabad, _____

b. _____ Sapporo, _____

_____ Tokyo, _____

_____ Shanghai, _____

_____ Munich, _____

_____ Santiago, _____

c. _____ London, _____

_____ Mexico City, _____

_____ New York, _____

_____ Beijing, _____

_____ Paris, _____

d. _____ Calcutta, _____

_____ Delhi, _____

_____ Baghdad, _____

_____ Canton, _____

_____ Shenyang, _____

e. _____ Hamburg, _____

_____ Istanbul, _____

_____ Chicago, _____

_____ Johannesburg, _____

_____ Sao Paulo, _____

f. _____ Los Angeles, _____

_____ Rome, _____

_____ Teheran, _____

_____ Moscow, _____

_____ Lima, _____

g. _____ Seoul, _____

_____ Tientsin, _____

_____ Karachi, _____

_____ Bombay, _____

_____ Cairo, _____

In the space below, list in descending order the world's ten largest cities with their populations.

GA1309

PROFILE OF A CITY

One of the greatest ways to get to know a city is to go there and experience its sights, sounds and smells firsthand. When that is impossible, the next best thing is to view a video or read about that city in books and magazines. Even if you are fortunate enough to actually visit the city, it's a good idea to do some research ahead of time. In that way you'll be certain to see all that you really want to see and won't miss anything you will regret once you've left the city.

To get you accustomed to this kind of research, choose one of the world's major cities from the list below which you would enjoy visiting and research the profile information required. You will be able to find much of the information you need from travel books, source books and magazines. But if you have the time, write to the Bureau of Travel and Tourism in the city of your choice, and they will send you, free of charge, flyers and brochures that will enrich your research and expand your knowledge.

Rio de Janeiro	Paris	Mexico City
New York	Johannesburg	Cairo
London	Los Angeles	Shanghai
Bombay	Tokyo	Moscow
Chicago	Berlin	Rome
Vienna	Sydney	Toronto
Buenos Aires	Singapore	Stockholm
Hong Kong	Seoul	São Paulo

GA1309

PROFILE OF A CITY

City:

Current Population:

Profile of the People (Ethnic Groups):

Language:

Historical Landmarks:

Other Important Symbols and Landmarks:

Parks and Playgrounds:

GA1309

PROFILE OF A CITY

Professional Sports and Recreation:

Amusements and Attractions:

Cultural Attractions:

Major Industries and Occupations:

Major Problems of Concern:

Create your own four-page 4" x 8½" folder that will attract visitors to the city of your choice. Include all the pluses you can that will highlight what the city has to offer. Include either rough drawings of your own or pictures that you cut from brochures and flyers. Create your own advertising copy to emphasize your points. Share your folders with other members of your class.

GA1309

CITY LANDMARKS

The attached page contains outlines of some of the world's most famous landmarks. Below is a list of those landmarks. The problem is that the letters are all scrambled. Your task is to unscramble the letters so that they make sense. Then match the letter corresponding to the city where each landmark is located.

1. _____ DETCAHRAL OF ST. SBAIL

   _____ __ _____

2. _____ YDNSEY POREA SUOHE

   _____ _____ _____

3. _____ NC RETWO

   __ _____

4. _____ ERAGT PSHIXN

   _____ _____

5. _____ ATJ AMHLA

   ____ _____

6. _____ LFIEFE ROTWE

   _____ _____

7. _____ ASTUET OF EBILTRY

   _____ __ _____

8. _____ NATPRHEON

   _____

9. _____ NEANLIG OETWR OF IPSA

   _____ _____ __ ____

10. _____ RASES WTOER

    _____ _____

11. _____ EALAPC OF ESEWTIMNSTR

    _____ __ _____

A. Paris, France

B. London, England

C. Sydney, Australia

D. New York City, USA

E. Moscow, Soviet Union

F. Toronto, Canada

G. Athens, Greece

H. Agra, India

I. Pisa, Italy

J. Giza, Egypt

K. Chicago, USA

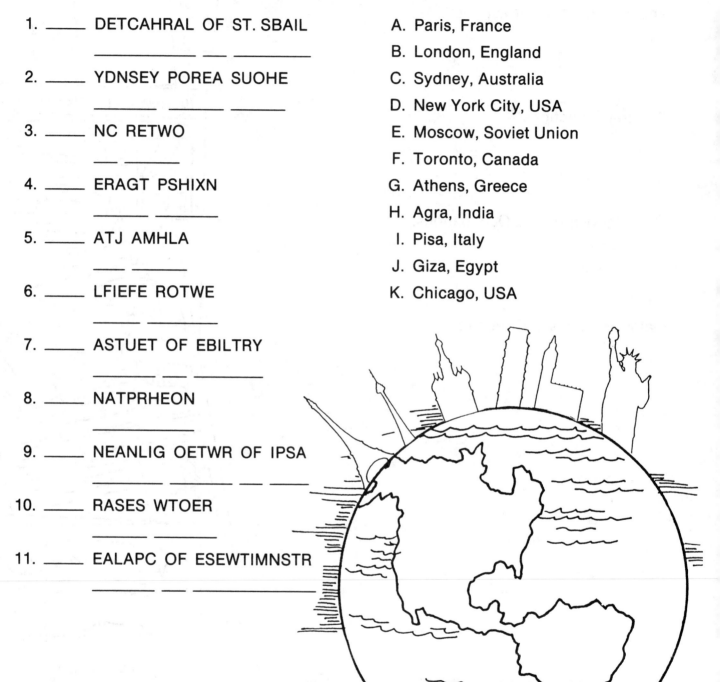

GA1309

CITY LANDMARKS

From the outlines below, identify each famous world landmark and write its name on the line provided.

1. _____

2. _____

3. _____

4. _____

5. _____

6. _____

7. _____

8. _____

9. _____

10. _____

11. _____

LOCATING THE WORLD'S GREAT CITIES

Each dot on the map represents the location of one of the world's great cities. Your task is to find from the list below the city that goes with each dot and neatly print the letter that corresponds to that city next to the dot.

a. Beijing
b. Seoul
c. São Paulo
d. Cape Town
e. Paris
f. Tokyo
g. Shanghai

h. New York
i. Cairo
j. London
k. Ho Chi Minh City
l. Jakarta
m. Lima
n. Sydney

o. Seattle
p. Toronto
q. Mexico City
r. Melbourne
s. Montreal
t. Chicago

u. Rio de Janeiro
v. Bombay
w. Los Angeles
x. Bogotá
y. Buenos Aires
z. Calcutta

aa. Berlin
bb. Johannesburg
cc. Delhi
dd. Rome
ee. Moscow
ff. Vienna

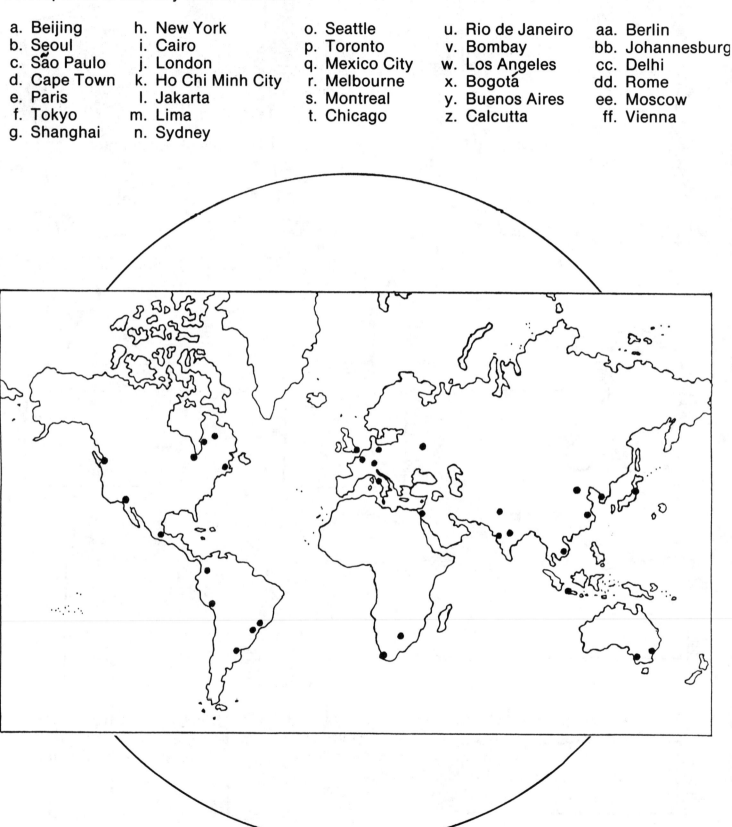

GA1309

CITIES IN THE NEWS

Bring to class clippings from ten articles you find in newspapers that have a major city in the headline of the story. Pinpoint the location of that city on a classroom wall map. Read each news article and jot down in the space below a statement that summarizes the reasons for the story's being newsworthy.

Headline   **Statement of Summary**

1. _____   _____

2. _____   _____

3. _____   _____

4. _____   _____

5. _____   _____

6. _____   _____

7. _____   _____

8. _____   _____

9. _____   _____

10. _____   _____

Go back through your list and decide which of the following categories best suits the description of each article: Political (P), Economic (E), Cultural (C), Social (S). Place the letter of the category you think best fits beside the number of each headline and share your choices with other members of your class.

GA1309

GLACIERS

More than two thirds of the world's fresh water is in the form of ice. Most of that frozen water is found on the continent of Antarctica in the form of *glaciers*. Glaciers are categorized either as Alpine glaciers which form on mountainsides and travel downward or as ice sheets which form on flat land and then spread out in all directions. The historical tract of glaciers is evident all over the world with the most pronounced effects seen in Europe and North America. During the Pleistocene period almost 20,000 years ago these ancient glaciers carved out much of the current landscape as we know it today. During that period over 30 percent of the earth's land surface was covered by glaciers. Today glaciers cover approximately 10 percent of the earth's land surface.

Glaciers are formed when the temperature is too cold to permit the accumulating snow to melt. As additional snow accumulates, the weight becomes heavy enough to compact the crystals of snow into granules. Additional compaction causes the formation of a grainy ice called *firn*. As this process continues, the mass accumulates into solid ice. Alpine glaciers then begin to move downward due to the force of gravity. The rate of movement varies within the glacier with the top part moving faster than the base. It is this grinding variance in movement that is mainly responsible for the dramatic changes glaciers bring about to the landscape. When glaciers reach the sea, chunks break off into the water and remain afloat as *icebergs*.

GA1309

THE WORLD'S LARGEST OUTDOOR LAB

ANTARCTICA

Antarctica, the fifth largest continent, is the coldest, most desolate place on earth. However, in recent years it has become a giant outdoor laboratory studied by scientists from many nations. It is indeed planet Earth's last frontier. The debate over the future of Antarctica remains a contested matter, but recorded history of exploration of the continent's secrets began only a few years ago. The U.S. Amundsen-Scott Station is the main base of most scientific explorations located at the South Pole. It is named in honor of the first two explorers to reach the South Pole.

Research the story behind this spirited competition and answer the following questions:

1. Who reached the South Pole first? Where was he from? When did he actually reach the South Pole? What was the reaction of his competitor?

_____

_____

_____

_____

2. In 1959 twelve nations signed the Antarctic Treaty, an agreement that no nation could claim ownership to Antarctica and that it would be used only for peaceful and scientific purposes. Since then thirteen other nations have signed the agreement. The agreement is currently up for review. Find out about the main issue of debate as this treaty is being reviewed.

_____

_____

_____

_____

3. It has been said that the Frozen Continent is a barometer of man's use and abuse of the planet Earth. Research the implications of this statement and discuss how Antarctica provides evidence that the earth's ozone layer has been damaged.

_____

_____

_____

_____

THE WORLD'S LARGEST OUTDOOR LAB

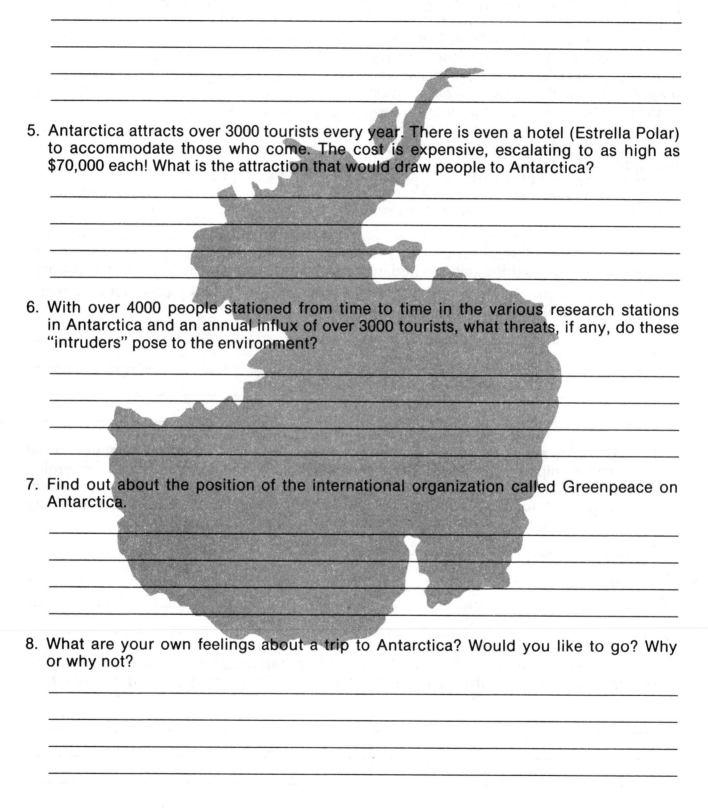

4. While there is a vast untapped wealth of minerals beneath Antarctica, there is also an abundance of wildlife. Find out about life on Antarctica and list some of the animal and plant life that exists.

_____

_____

_____

_____

5. Antarctica attracts over 3000 tourists every year. There is even a hotel (Estrella Polar) to accommodate those who come. The cost is expensive, escalating to as high as $70,000 each! What is the attraction that would draw people to Antarctica?

_____

_____

_____

_____

6. With over 4000 people stationed from time to time in the various research stations in Antarctica and an annual influx of over 3000 tourists, what threats, if any, do these "intruders" pose to the environment?

_____

_____

_____

_____

7. Find out about the position of the international organization called Greenpeace on Antarctica.

_____

_____

_____

_____

8. What are your own feelings about a trip to Antarctica? Would you like to go? Why or why not?

_____

_____

_____

_____

GA1309

PRECIPITATION

Water is so essential to life that it makes up approximately three fourths of all living things. It is continually recycled between the sea, the air and the land. When it returns to earth from the atmosphere, it is called *precipitation*. That precipitation can fall in the form of rain, sleet, snow or hail, depending on its temperature. While precipitation is life-sustaining, it can also bring tragedy, financial ruin and even death.

Precipitation does not fall all over the earth in equal yearly amounts. There are deserts where less than a half inch of rain falls in an entire year. There are also rain forests where precipitation can exceed 400 inches (1016 cm) per year! What causes this wide variation? First of all, precipitation falls to earth from clouds. We know that clouds are formed when warm moist air rises and cools. There are then other factors that enter into what happens to those clouds once they have been formed.

There are basically three causes of rising air. Those causes are *convection*, *orographic lifting* and the movement of weather fronts.

Below and on the next page are drawings that illustrate the formation of each of these causes for precipitation. Investigate how each is created and then label the cause and write a brief explanation in the blank space provided.

1. Cause: _____

   Explanation: _____

   _____

   _____

   _____

   _____

   _____

   _____

   _____

Warm Air

111

GA1309

PRECIPITATION

Warm Moist Air

Cold Air

Warm Moist Air

2. Cause: _____

   Explanation: _____

   _____

   _____

   _____

   _____

   _____

   _____

   _____

3. Cause: _____

   Explanation: _____

   _____

   _____

   _____

   _____

   _____

   _____

   _____

   _____

While precipitation is essential to life, it can also bring about disaster and tragedy. Beside each form of precipitation listed below, cite an example of that form of precipitation that can be beneficial to mankind (if there is one) and also an example of destruction or tragedy that can be a result of the same form of precipitation.

Precipitation	Good	Bad
Rain		
Snow		
Sleet		
Hail		
Fog		

GA1309

WATER CYCLE

One of the cycles in nature that is essential to life on earth is the water cycle. The constant change and exchange within the cycle makes all living things live and grow. Listed below are the steps and exchanges that make up a typical water cycle. They are, however, not listed in any particular order. In the drawing below the list, show your own knowledge of how the water cycle works. Label all areas and events that are a part of the list in their proper sequence and use directional arrows to help with your explanation.

Water drains into lakes
Plants use water from the soil
Water vapor cools and forms clouds
Sun heats bodies of water, causing evaporation
Animals and plants return water to the soil when they die and decompose
Clouds meet cold air as they are forced up mountains
Water flows down mountain streams
Precipitation falls to earth as rain or snow

Create Your Own Water Cycle

Place about an inch of water in a plastic bowl. Cover the bowl with a plastic wrap and seal with a rubber band. Set the bowl in the sun. The heat will evaporate the water, which will then rise and collect on the plastic. As it cools, it will condense and fall back into the container as rain.

GA1309

RAINFALL AROUND THE WORLD

On the back of this map (or on another sheet of paper) write down ten statements that are true conclusions you can draw by looking at the information contained on the map. Share your list with other members of your class.

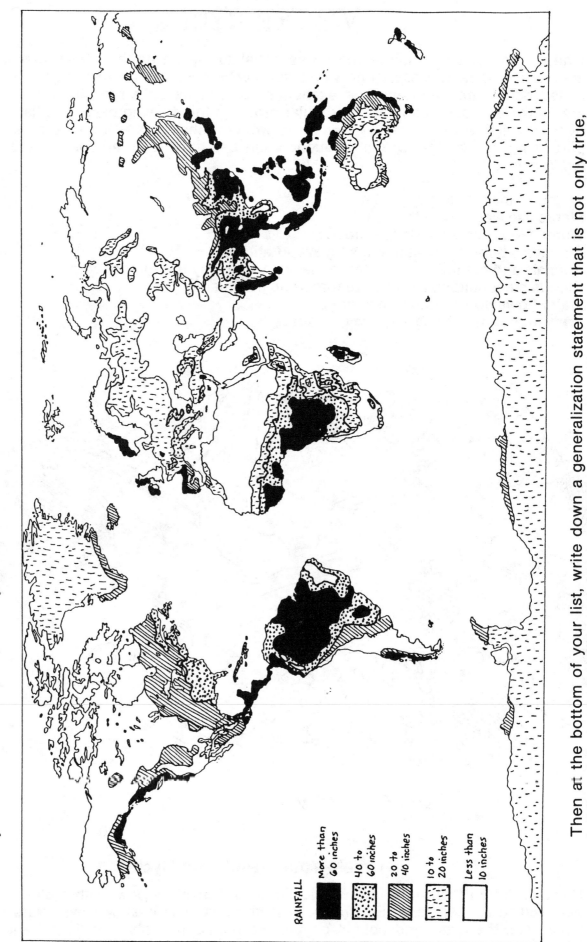

RAINFALL

More than 60 inches

40 to 60 inches

20 to 40 inches

10 to 20 inches

Less than 10 inches

Then at the bottom of your list, write down a generalization statement that is not only true, but is a statement you will remember tomorrow.

GA1309

SOIL

The surface of the earth is covered with layers of soil. In looking at a cross section of soil, it is easy to see the various layers as they exist. The width of these layers and the composition of the soil itself varies from one soil to another and from one area to another. Soil samples taken within even a few feet of each other can vary a great deal in composition and texture.

Soils are made up of varying amounts of air, water, minerals and organic matter that is composed of decayed plant and animal remains. The soils of our earth provide nutrition for the grasses, the farm crops and the forests which grow above them. The texture of a soil affects the nutrition supply it can provide plants and living things. Texture is determined by the size of the minerals contained in the soil. Those with a high content of sand dry quickly and thus are not very fertile. The most fertile of soils are the *loams*, which contain appropriate quantities of sand, silt and clay to hold moisture, but still allow for easy cultivation.

Color provides another clue to a soil's fertility. For example, *humus* is an organic material that helps to make the soil fertile, and humus soil is very dark in color. Red soil, on the other hand, sometimes indicates soil that has been washed of its minerals and thus lacks fertility.

A Slice of Soil

Below is a cross section drawing of a soil profile. The various layers that can be visibly distinguished within the sample are called *horizons*.

The various layers shown are described but are out of their proper order. Look at the drawing and use the correct name of its horizon to identify each.

_____ layer beyond reach of plants, contains material from bedrocks

_____ organic material that either decomposed or did not decompose

_____ layer containing minerals dissolved from decayed plants

_____ layer containing clay and iron that is poor for growing plants

115

GA1309

EROSION AND CONSERVATION

The forces of nature and the intervention of man have combined to bring about the relocation of billions of tons of the earth's best soil. Wind, the force of gravity and floodwaters are responsible for moving soil far from its original location. Sometimes this is beneficial to mankind, but more often is the case of this relocation bringing about a hardship to man.

Human activity can accelerate the pace of erosion by causing excessive losses of topsoil. Anytime erosion occurs to a degree, ecosystems are disrupted. The damming of rivers, the plowing of fields and the cutting down of forests are all examples of human activity that result in erosion. Below are some thought-provoking questions that will help you to better identify the problems and to decide on solutions.

1. In many of the underdeveloped nations, farmers are planting crops on steeply sloped lands that lead to severe erosion. Others in dry nations plow land that is simply blown away by winds. What can be done to lessen the effects of these poor farming methods?

   _____

   _____

   _____

   _____

   _____

2. When crop yields decline, the cause is oftentimes traced to soil that has lost some of its fertility. This in many cases is because of an overuse of the soil. The results can be devastating to nations that become dependent upon high-yield farming. What can be done to stop this overuse and thus prevent the widespread famime and starvation that are often the result?

   _____

   _____

   _____

   _____

   _____

3. Soil is sometimes lost when highways, shopping malls, airports and home sites are built. Land erodes and washes or blows away because the natural vegetation is lost. What can be done to lessen the loss of soil through such construction?

   _____

   _____

   _____

   _____

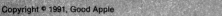

GA1309

CLIMATE

The sum total of all the weather conditions that create consistent patterns over a period of time in an area become known as that area's *climate*. People often use the terms *climate* and *weather* synonomously, but they really have different meanings. Very simply, weather is the condition of the atmosphere over a short period of time, whereas climate is the expected condition over a much longer, seasonal period of time.

There are a number of factors that combine to give us a broad picture of predictability on the climate of a given area. The amount of annual precipitation and the state in which it falls is certainly one of the factors that enters into the broad definition of the climate a particular area has.

Temperature is another consideration in defining an area's climate. The average highs and lows recorded over a given period of time for a specific time of year eventually become the expectations of the future during the same time. Other factors that affect climate are topography, the kind of vegetation found and the location of the area relative to large bodies of water. As a result of all this, those who live there adapt their living habits to make their environment more comfortable. In the case of human beings, we can buy clothing that is appropriate and comfortable for the season. With animals and plants, the adaptation must come from nature itself.

GA1309

CHANGING CLIMATES

While most climatic changes have occurred over extended periods of time (thousands of years), there have been some changes in more recent times that spanned only a brief period of a few years. Examples are El Niño, sunspots on the surface of the sun and the greenhouse effect. Research each and jot down how these forces can have an effect on our climate.

El Niño: _____

_____

_____

Sunspots: _____

_____

_____

Greenhouse Effect: _____

_____

_____

Climate of the Future?

1. Many climatologists are concerned about the long-range implications the greenhouse effect will have on the climate of the earth. If the temperature rises, speculate on how this might affect the polar regions of the world.

_____

_____

_____

2. What are some other predictions you can make that might well be a direct result of the ice caps melting?

_____

_____

_____

3. How can human activity help to bring about a reduction of the greenhouse effect?

_____

_____

_____

4. Why does it get colder as you climb up a mountain when you are really getting closer to the sun?

_____

_____

_____

GA1309

OUR MAJOR CLIMATES

Below are classifications and descriptions of the major climates we experience in various places all over the planet Earth. Read each description and then place its corresponding letter in the blank space beside the name of the climate that it best describes.

1. _____ Polar Climates

2. _____ Dry Climates

3. _____ Mild Climates

4. _____ Continental Climates

5. _____ Mountain Climates

6. _____ Tropical Climates

a. Located between mild and polar climates, this climate is influenced most by latitudes and landforms.

b. Precipitation is scarce and temperature changes are dramatic and can occur quickly.

c. Climates located in the lower latitudes on either side of the equator; temperatures are hot the year around.

d. Climates that are affected by both latitude and the warm water of the oceans. These climates have a pronounced effect on the land areas nearby.

e. climates where summers are very short and only the hardiest of plants and animals can survive

f. climates that are most directly affected by altitude

When you have finished matching the climates to their descriptions, cite an example where each climate is found.

GA1309

CLIMATES AROUND THE WORLD

The climate map which you will use for this activity has a slightly different classification of climates than the one you used for the activity "Our Major Climates." Locate on your map of the world each of the following places. Then indicate in the blank space the kind of climate found there.

1. Australian Outback _____

2. Chicago, Illinois _____

3. São Paulo _____

4. Algeria _____

5. Greenland _____

6. Mexico City _____

7. Rome _____

8. Saudi Arabia _____

9. Amazon Interior _____

10. Liberia _____

11. Cheyenne, Wyoming _____

12. Sydney, Australia _____

13. Caracas, Venezuela _____

14. Toronto _____

15. Indonesia _____

16. Southern California _____

17. Helsinki, Finland _____

18. Moscow, U.S.S.R. _____

19. Fairbanks, Alaska _____

20. Mongolia _____

CLIMATES AROUND THE WORLD

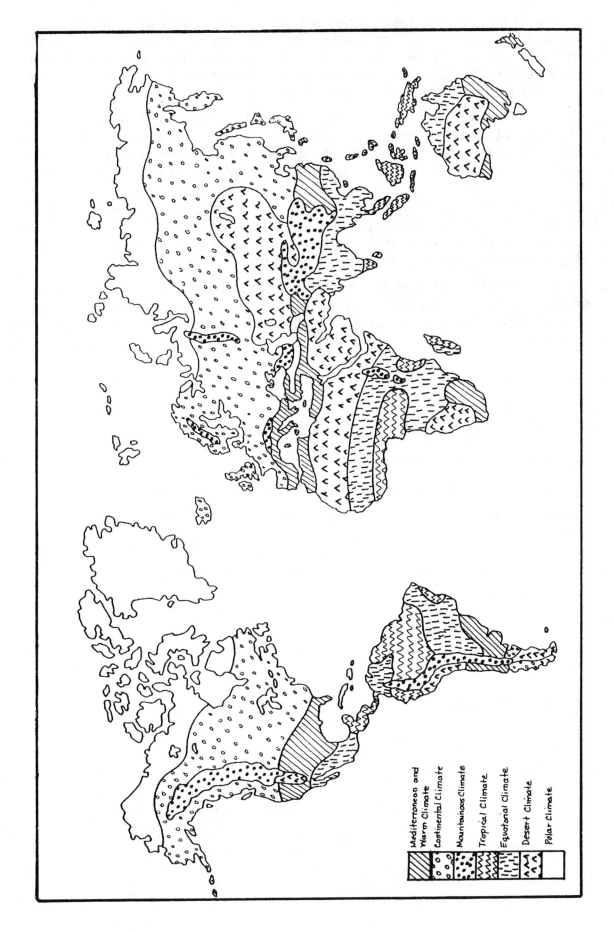

Mediterranean and Warm Climate
Continental Climate
Mountainous Climate
Tropical Climate
Equatorial Climate
Desert Climate
Polar Climate

GA1309

POPULATION

The number of people who live in a defined area is that area's *population*. That number will change from time to time, depending on the number of people who move in and out and by both the birth and death rates of that area. The people who study these trends are called *demographers*. Studying such trends is very important in helping to plan for an area's future needs, its problems and desires.

Perhaps the most important information gathered for use by those who are studying a specific area is that area's *census*, an official head count that is conducted on a periodic basis. During a census the government makes every attempt possible to count all of the people who live in an area or governmental unit. In addition they usually ask the inhabitants a few simple questions that will provide meaningful data to the demographers who will study that area. Finding out where the people live and why they live there will be useful for those who help to plan for the future of that area. Because overpopulation is a major problem in certain parts of the world, it is important for us to examine some of the tools and techniques used by demographers.

If you yourself were in charge of conducting a census of the city or town where you live, one of your main concerns would be to make certain that all of the people are counted. What steps would you take to implement a policy that made certain everyone was included?

_____

_____

_____

_____

_____

_____

_____

_____

_____

_____

GA1309

PEOPLE COUNTING

Asking pertinent questions of those included is also a very important part of any census. Think of the kinds of information you would want to include and the value that such data can provide. In the space below jot down the kinds of information you would want to gather.

_____

_____

_____

_____

Below is space for creating a questionnaire that you would use in conducting your census. Make certain your questions are clear, concise and will lead to the kinds of information you can tabulate. Limit the number of questions you ask to seven.

While demographers are interested in many facts about the lives of people who live in the area they are studying, they must be careful to avoid asking questions that are an invasion of privacy. What are some questions that should *not* be included in a census questionnaire because encouraging people to answer them would be an invasion of privacy? Are any of your questions such a violation of privacy?

DEMOGRAPHIC DILEMMAS

Demographers are very much interested in population growths and trends because both the environment and the balance of nature are today being threatened by overpopulation. It took several thousand years for the earth's population to reach 1 billion (1930's). It took only another century to reach the second billion. By the year 1975 the earth had increased its population to 4 billion. It then took a mere twelve years (1975-1987) to grow another billion!

Below are eight statements that are true and contain some very significant information to the people who make a living by analyzing such information. Read each carefully; then choose four that you feel are important and speculate on what you think the implications mean for each one. Identify each choice you make by jotting down its letter in front of your statement(s).

a. Populations are usually the densest along the coastlines.

b. India has more people than all the Western Hemisphere plus Australia combined.

c. Areas that are densely populated usually have features in common that make them appealing to people.

d. In developing countries the trends in population shifts are usually from the rural areas to the city.

e. Almost a half billion people go to bed hungry every night.

f. Population problems are contributing to other environmental issues that help to increase worldwide tension.

g. A major part of the population problem is the unequal sharing of the earth's resources between rich and poor nations.

h. It is felt that the population of the world will level out at around 10 billion by the end of the next century.

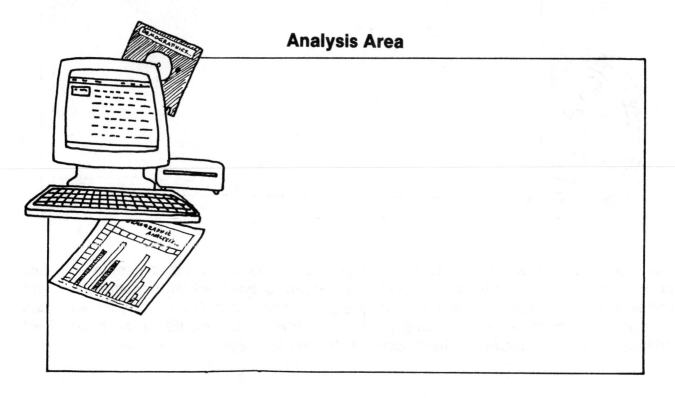

Analysis Area

COMPARING CONTINENTS

Land Area

Approximately three fourths of the earth's surface (75%) is covered by water. That means that only 25 percent remains for the land that is the home of the earth's 5 billion people. To the right is a circle graph that shows graphically how much of the whole land area each continent contains.

To calculate how this graph was constructed, use a protractor to measure the number of degrees in each segment of the pie. For example, the segment marked Asia occupies 108° of the circle graph. Then divide 108 by 360 (the number of degrees in the whole circle), and you should get 30 percent. You could say then that Asia occupies 30 percent of the earth's land area. Calculate the other continents in the same manner and place the number of degrees and the calculated percentage in the space provided.

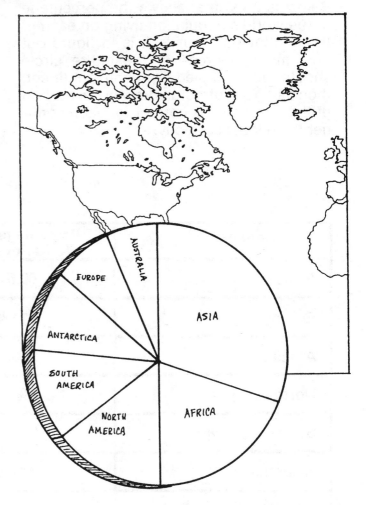

Continent	Number of Degrees	Calculated Percentage of Earth's Land Area
Asia	108°	30%
Africa		
North America		
South America		
Antarctica		
Europe		
Australia		

GA1309

COMPARING CONTINENTS

Below is a list that shows the percentage of the world's population living on each of the continents. Your task is to figure out how many degrees of the entire circle should be occupied by each continent; then using a protractor, draw in the portion of the circle that is correct for each continent and label correctly.

Population of Continents

Continents	Percentage of the World Population	Number of Degrees
Asia	60.5%	
Europe	13.5%	
Africa	12%	
North America	8%	
South America	5.5%	
Australia	.5%	
Antarctica	0%	

If the earth has appoximately 5 billion people, how many live on each continent?

Asia _____

Europe_____

Africa_____

North America_____

South America _____

Australia_____

Antarctica_____

From the information you have learned and calculated over these two pages, make five general statements of your choice that you can make about the population distribution of the world as it relates to the continents.

_____

_____

_____

_____

_____

GA1309

THE POPULATION OF ASIA

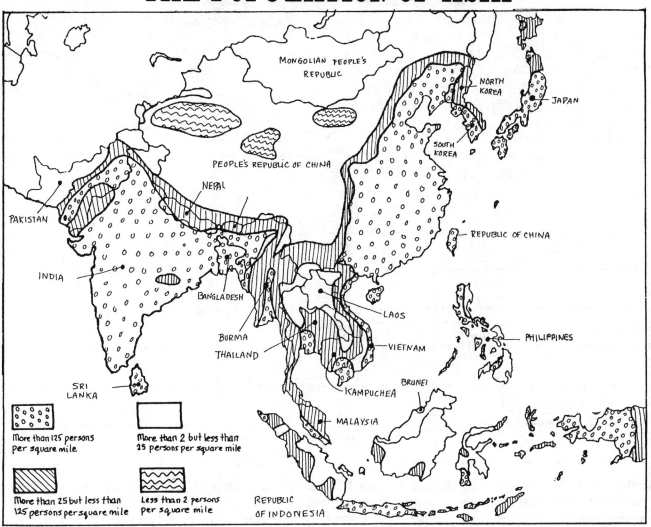

1. According to the information provided by the map, which countries in Asia have the greatest population?

_____

_____

_____

_____

2. Why do you think Asia has such densely populated areas?

_____

_____

_____

_____

3. In the midst of such densely populated areas, there are a few areas that show very few people per square mile. Why don't some of the people in the heavily populated areas move to these areas where they would be less crowded?

_____

_____

_____

GA1309

ENERGY

Energy is the capacity to do work. Our bodies need energy to make them function and perform the routine tasks of daily living. Energy is also needed to cook our food, heat and cool our homes and power the planes, trains and automobiles that move us from one place to another.

Throughout history man has been dependent upon wood, mining, water and wind to provide him with energy to help him to do his work and to make his life more comfortable and convenient. Where does all this energy come from? Most of the energy that is used on the planet Earth comes from the sun. The heat and light that radiate to the earth warm the atmosphere which in turn causes wind. The sun also evaporates water in the oceans and large bodies of water. As the moisture rises, it cools, condenses and falls as rain, where it drains into the rivers that are controlled by dams that turn the moving water into electric power.

Even the fossil fuels which currently serve as our major source of energy once had their beginnnings with the sun's energy. The decomposed and animal remains out of which they developed thousands of years ago once lived because of the sun. The sad news is that this once vast source of energy is fast being depleted. Fossil fuels are irreplaceable, and our current rate of use compared with existing supplies has made us painfully aware that other energy sources must be found.

Fortunately other sources are available and current research continues to explore other avenues. Our future supplies of energy will become increasingly dependent upon a combination of finding new and efficient energy sources and conserving what we have.

A SLICE OF ENERGY

Below is a graph showing a recent breakdown of the world's current energy sources. Look closely at the information it provides to answer the questions that follow.

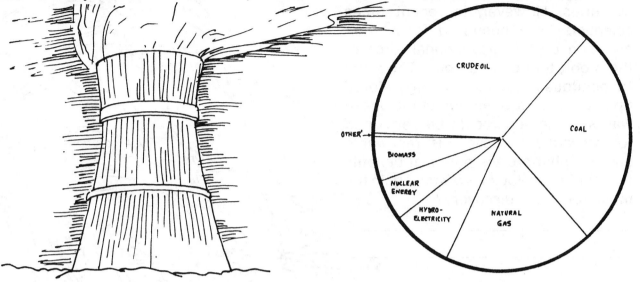

1. Measure with your protractor to find the number of degrees each segment of the circle occupies and indicate in the space below.

   Crude Oil ＿＿＿

   Coal ＿＿＿

   Natural Gas ＿＿＿

   Hydroelectricity ＿＿＿

   Biomass ＿＿＿

   Nuclear Energy ＿＿＿

   Other ＿＿＿

   Does the sum of your calculations above add up to 360? It should!

2. Now calculate the approximate percentage of the whole circle each segment occupies. To do this, divide the number of degrees you measured in each segment by 360. Your answer should be expressed as a percent.

   Crude Oil ＿＿＿

   Coal ＿＿＿

   Natural Gas ＿＿＿

   Hydroelectricity ＿＿＿

   Biomass ＿＿＿

   Nuclear Energy ＿＿＿

   Other ＿＿＿

3. What conclusions can you draw based on this information? Jot down at least three.

   _____

   _____

   _____

"WAVE" OF THE FUTURE

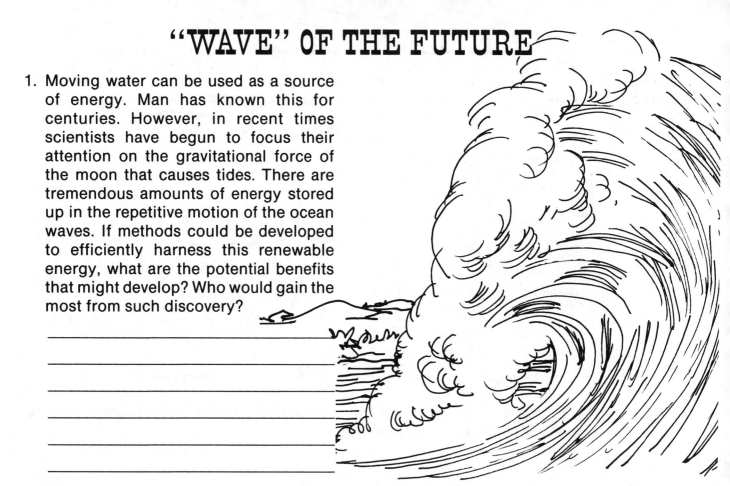

1. Moving water can be used as a source of energy. Man has known this for centuries. However, in recent times scientists have begun to focus their attention on the gravitational force of the moon that causes tides. There are tremendous amounts of energy stored up in the repetitive motion of the ocean waves. If methods could be developed to efficiently harness this renewable energy, what are the potential benefits that might develop? Who would gain the most from such discovery?

   _____

   _____

   _____

   _____

   _____

   _____

2. Corn is now more than just a food product. Find out how it is being used to help provide a new source of energy.

   _____

   _____

   _____

   _____

3. Find out about the role of "solar farms" in the future of our energy needs.

   _____

   _____

   _____

   _____

4. Find out the latest on *photovoltaics* and explain how they may help to give us clean, affordable energy in the future.

   _____

   _____

   _____

   _____

GA1309

SEARCHING FOR NATURE'S TREASURES

Hidden in the letters below are the names of thirty of our natural wonders. Each of nature's finest in the list below is located somewhere in the maze of letters. Some names are found as we read—from left to right. Others are in reverse or located vertically. Your task is to find each and circle the letters that make up the name of the natural wonder. Then name the continent on which it is located in the blank next to the name of the wonder in the list.

```
A E T I D S L L A F H C A B B U A T S N K G
S O V G E K A L T L A S T A E R G E C I C I
L L G R W M T M C K I N L E Y B A O H G O A
L D N A M A Z O N O E K A L R E T A R C R N
A F R N R E B U N A D U D I J U F T M T S T
F A O D V G A N G E S L E N I H R M N O R S
A I H C M O N T B L A N C I T E R O E O E C
R T R A E T D E A T H V A L L E Y A T B Y A
A H E N O S M V I C T O R I A F A L L S A U
G F T Y P G R E A T B A R R I E R R E E F S
A U T O I F O R S L L A F U C A U G I W X E
I L A N O S A E S D A E D K A S E H K Y A W
N Y M D R O S S I C E S H E L F H O T I H A
E Z T G N A Y T S N I G E R P T N T R A W Y
S N A I R O T C I V E K A L S U P M Y L O X
S U G A R L O A F M O U N T A I N A D L O U
```

1. Olympus _____
2. Iguacú Falls _____
3. Amazon _____
4. Mount Everest _____
5. Ganges _____
6. Death Valley _____
7. Mont Blanc _____
8. Dead Sea _____
9. Alps _____
10. Niger _____
11. Victoria Falls _____
12. Grand Canyon _____
13. Ross Ice Shelf _____
14. Mt. McKinley _____
15. Matterhorn _____

16. Great Barrier Reef _____
17. Nile _____
18. Crater Lake _____
19. Yangtze _____
20. Staubbach Falls _____
21. Sugarloaf Mountain _____
22. Danube _____
23. Lake Victoria _____
24. Old Faithful _____
25. Great Salt Lake _____
26. Mt. Fuji _____
27. Rhine _____
28. Ayers Rock _____
29. Niagara Falls _____
30. Giant's Causeway _____

GA1309

NATURE'S TREASURES

The natural wonders of the earth are just that—products of nature that bring to earth spectacular scenery or are unique because of the geological phenomena behind their creation. Millions of people spend billions of dollars annually travelling all over the world to visit these treasures of nature. Families often plan their entire vacations around them. Place the name of one of the natural wonders found on each of the continents below beside the name of that continent.

_____ Asia _____

_____ Africa _____

_____ North America _____

_____ South America _____

_____ Europe _____

_____ Australia _____

Go back through your list and rank order the natural wonders in the order of your preference.

In the space below write the names of ten natural wonders you would like to visit. Beside each give a reason for your choice.

_____

_____

_____

_____

_____

_____

_____

_____

_____

_____

Choose the single wonder of our world you would personally rather visit than any other. Research the geological phenomena behind its formation and report your findings on the back side of this page.

GA1309

NATURE'S WONDERS

As we begin to look closely at the natural wonders of nature that are found on this earth, we begin to develop a greater appreciation of the powerful, yet delicate. . .simple, and complex force that it truly is. Below are the scrambled names of several of the world's natural wonders. Use the hint to the right of each to help you solve each scramble. Write the name of each wonder in the first blank(s) under each wonder. The second line is reserved for you to jot down the continent on which it is found.

1. AIRCVITO SLFAL

_____ _____
_____

Where the Zambezi River plummets suddenly over 350 feet (106 m) straight down.

2. NAGRD NYCNAO

_____ _____
_____

The world's largest canyon, it measures up to 18 miles (29 km) across and is a mile deep in places.

3. OSSR CIE LSEFH

_____ ___ _____
_____

Largest ice shelf in the world, it covers over 200,000 square miles (518,000 sq. km) and is over 2000 feet (600 m) thick.

4. YAKLBA

_____
_____

The world's deepest lake

5. TUOMN UFJI

_____ _____
_____

A dormant volcano in Japan, it has been a sacred mountain to those of the Shinto religion

6. RTEGA RARREBI EREF

_____ _____ _____
_____

Home of the most diverse array of fauna anywhere, it is the world's longest reef, extending over 1200 miles (1935 km).

7. NGLAE SLLFA

_____ _____
_____

The world's highest waterfall, with its waters plummeting over 3000 feet (900 m) into a jungle canyon below

8. UNVATAJKOLL

_____
_____

This huge glacier covers almost 10 percent of Iceland.

9. WIESEIRSENELT

_____
_____

Caverns that include the earth's largest known ice cave

GA1309

NATURE'S WONDERS

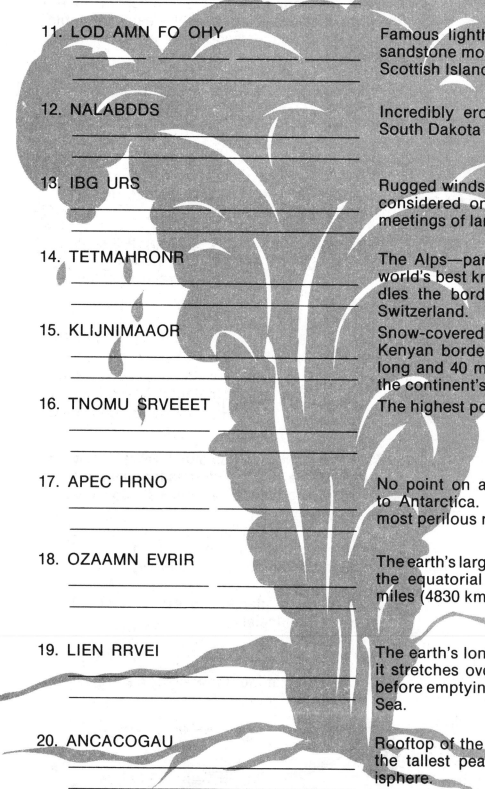

10. RAGUSFALO ATNOMUIN

_____ _____

_____

Famous landmark near Rio de Janeiro

11. LOD AMN FO OHY

_____ _____ _____

_____

Famous lighthouse without a light, a sandstone monolith off the coast of the Scottish Island of Hoy

12. NALABDDS

_____

_____

Incredibly eroded plateau in western South Dakota

13. IBG URS

_____

_____

Rugged windswept California coastline considered one of the most dramatic meetings of land and crashing sea

14. TETMAHRONR

_____

_____

The Alps—par excellence—one of the world's best known mountains, it straddles the border between France and Switzerland.

15. KLIJNIMAAOR

_____

_____

Snow-covered summit in Tanzania near Kenyan border, it is 40 miles (64 km) long and 40 miles (64 km) wide and is the continent's tallest mountain.

16. TNOMU SRVEEET

_____

_____

The highest point on the planet

17. APEC HRNO

_____

_____

No point on any continent lies closer to Antarctica. It is one of the world's most perilous maritime routes.

18. OZAAMN EVRIR

_____

_____

The earth's largest river, it glides through the equatorial jungle for almost 3000 miles (4830 km).

19. LIEN RRVEI

_____

_____

The earth's longest, most historic river, it stretches over 4100 miles (6600 km) before emptying into the Mediterranean Sea.

20. ANCACOGAU

_____

_____

Rooftop of the Andes, this mountain is the tallest peak in the Western Hemisphere.

When you have identified the natural wonders called for in this scramble, mark the location of each on your outline map of the world by placing the corresponding number in the proper location.

PEOPLES OF THE WORLD

There are over 150 countries on earth that vary in population count from a few hundred people to hundreds of millions. Each of these countries is unique with its own customs and traditions. The language spoken by the people of a country to communicate with each other may be different from that of a neighboring country. Often it is the case in a larger country that several different languages will be spoken by various peoples that also have different belief systems. The assignments and tasks found in this short unit will help you to understand the individual characteristics that combine to give a country its own unique "personality." Those qualities make it different from all other countries.

Included in that unique flavoring are these essentials: the type of government; the language spoken by the people; the religion and systems of beliefs followed by the majority of people; their ancestoral background; their medium of exchange; their socioeconomic status; and the customs, traditions, music, dance and special celebrations cherished most by those who live there. It is the sum total of all these characteristics that make a country what it is.

As human beings, we have common needs that are essential to our survival. How we go about satisfying those needs varies, but the common ground was established long ago. Perhaps learning more about how others in foreign lands live will help us to better understand and appreciate the differences that do exist.

GA1309

LANGUAGE

With over 4000 languages spoken in the world today, the study of different languages is an overwhelming (but fascinating) one indeed. Over 1000 languages are spoken on the continents of Africa alone! Languages range in complexity from Chinese, which has over 40,000 written characters, to some of the tribal languages in Africa, which have no written form at all.

The set of sounds and letters which make the words of various languages are called that language's alphabet. These also vary from a few simple symbols to those languages that are complex and require thousands of characters that stand for parts of words. Most languages are read from left to right, but here again there are differences. Arabic, for example, is read from right to left.

People who study languages have grouped them into what are called *language families*. Certain common characteristics are found among all languages that are within each language group. Location and history also play major roles in the language spoken by a particular country.

To get you started in your research on the language of other lands, state the following sentence in any language. . .other than English: Studying people of other nations helps us to better understand that the differences among us are small.

_____

_____

_____

_____

_____

_____

Now create a message of your own in a foreign language other than the one you used above. Then exchange messages with another student and interpret each other's messages.

_____

_____

_____

_____

_____

_____

LANGUAGE

Your task in the activity below is to match the country with the language spoken in that country. Some will be easy; others may require a bit of research. Some countries have more than one language.

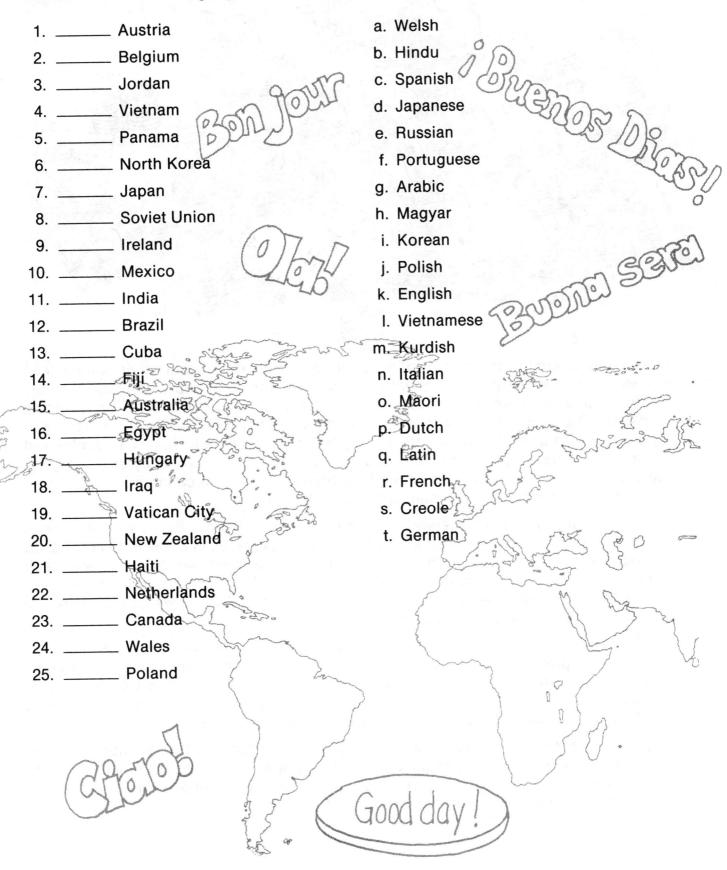

1. _____ Austria
2. _____ Belgium
3. _____ Jordan
4. _____ Vietnam
5. _____ Panama
6. _____ North Korea
7. _____ Japan
8. _____ Soviet Union
9. _____ Ireland
10. _____ Mexico
11. _____ India
12. _____ Brazil
13. _____ Cuba
14. _____ Fiji
15. _____ Australia
16. _____ Egypt
17. _____ Hungary
18. _____ Iraq
19. _____ Vatican City
20. _____ New Zealand
21. _____ Haiti
22. _____ Netherlands
23. _____ Canada
24. _____ Wales
25. _____ Poland

a. Welsh
b. Hindu
c. Spanish
d. Japanese
e. Russian
f. Portuguese
g. Arabic
h. Magyar
i. Korean
j. Polish
k. English
l. Vietnamese
m. Kurdish
n. Italian
o. Maori
p. Dutch
q. Latin
r. French
s. Creole
t. German

Bon jour

¡Buenos Dias!

Ola!

Buona sera

Ciao!

Good day!

MONEY

Anything that people agree to accept in exchange for the goods and services they need and want is called *money*. Most countries today use a form of paper certificates called *currency*. Smaller denominations of the money are often found in the form of coins or tokens. The value of a country's money can vary from one day to the next and is dependent upon a number of factors. Money brings a certain stability to a country and to the lives of the people who own it. Being aware of how much money one has gives that person a fairly accurate idea of the time frame in which he can continue to satisfy his needs. Such forecasting and planning is called a *budget*.

Man has not always used currency as the medium of exchange. Beads and shells and even fishhooks have all been used at one time in various places in the world in exchange for goods and services. Before that people simply struck their own bargains with each other. If one party had something wanted by another in exchange for something he owned, the two could close a deal. Such exchanging is called *bartering*, and there are still places where some of this occurs.

In more recent times, gold and silver became the acceptable standard of exchange of their value as precious metals. Even today with each country having its own currency, gold is bought and sold daily in various money markets all over the world. Its price can vary from day to day much like the stock exchange. The big factors are demand and the current value of the country's currency being offered in exchange.

Even though each country has its own currency, the values attached are not the same. Thus, when travelling from one country to another, people must have their money changed into the country's currency in which they will be travelling. Those people involved in changing the currency charge a fee for their services.

MONEY

Below are the names of several different currencies. Your task is to unscramble the letters, and then match each to the country in which it is used.

1. ____ Venezuela	_____	a. ARIDN
2. ____ Soviet Union	_____	b. AILR
3. ____ Canada	_____	c. ALABBO
4. ____ Mexico	_____	d. NUAY
5. ____ China	_____	e. NEY
6. ____ Netherlands	_____	f. KAMR
7. ____ West Germany	_____	g. SOEP
8. ____ Italy	_____	h. RLODLA
9. ____ Japan	_____	i. CAFRN
10. ____ Iraq	_____	j. UIDGRLE
11. ____ France	_____	k. BURLE
12. ____ Panama	_____	l. BAVILOR

The value of a country and currency varies from one day to the next. Such fluctuations are caused by a number of factors. Choose a country, investigate its currency and discuss in the space below the reasons behind the value of its currency varying in the world market.

_____

_____

_____

_____

_____

There are still places on earth where people live in such primitive surroundings that they have no money with which to buy the goods and services that are so valuable to our lives and well being. For a moment, think of yourself in such a situation. Imagine yourself living somewhere in the Kalahari Desert in Africa. How would you survive? What adjustments would be necessary for you to make?

_____

_____

_____

_____

_____

GA1309

MONEY CHANGERS

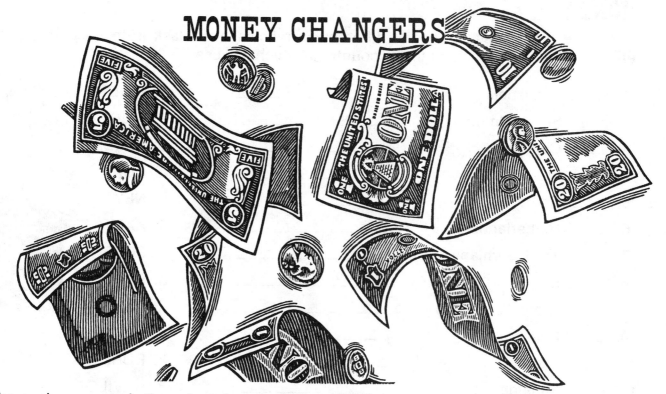

The exchange rate is the price of one country's currency as measured by that of another. The rates of exchange vary from day to day. Below are several problems that relate to a typical money exchange. Look carefully at the information provided; then calculate the math in the space provided that will lead to the current answer.

1. If the Canadian dollar is valued at $.815 in U.S. dollars, how much in U.S. currency would it take to buy $100 in Canadian currency? _____

2. If the German mark is valued at $.435 in U.S. dollars, how many marks could one get for $50 U.S. dollars? _____

3. If there are 247.8 Japanese yen per U.S. dollar, what is the value of $500 U.S. dollars in yen? _____

4. If the value of the Indian rupee is $.108 in U.S. dollars, how many rupees are there in a U.S. dollar? _____

5. If 10.37 Mexican pesos can be bought for a U.S. dollar, what is the value of a single peso in U.S. currency? _____

6. If there are 1310.6 Italian lira for the value of a U.S. dollar, how much would a jacket valued at $120 cost in an Italian fashion shop that accepts lira? _____

7. If a Russian ruble is worth $1.40 in U.S. dollars, how many rubles does a car cost that is made in the United States and valued at $12,800 U.S. dollars? _____

8. If the South African rand is valued at $.950 in U.S. dollars, how much in rands does a U.S. tennis racket valued at $89.95 (U.S. dollars) cost? _____

9. If the Swiss franc is valued at $.517 U.S. dollars, how much in U.S. dollars would a Swiss watch cost that is marked 2500 francs? _____

10. In China the yuan is worth $.557 in U.S. dollars. How much in yuan does a night's stay cost in a hotel that charges $84.95 (U.S. dollars) per night? _____

ETHNIC FLAVOR

We know that food is the basic fuel that provides us with the energy we need to nurture growth and sustain life. The kinds of different foods eaten by people all over the world varies a great deal, dependent upon a number of factors—availability, socioeconomic status and cultural background. The rich multicultural variety of our earth becomes quite obvious when looking at ethnic foods. Some of these foods are such gastronomical delights that they are important "staples" among the people in the country where they originated and are considered gourmet foods by others all over the world. Below are the names of some of those foods that have reached that distinction status. Trace the culture to the origin of each and place the name of that country in the space beside each food.

1. veal cordon bleu _____
2. chicken kiev _____
3. frankfurter _____
4. spaghetti _____
5. chop suey _____
6. chicken teriyaki _____
7. soufflé _____
8. tortillas _____
9. antipasto _____
10. sauerkraut _____
11. pizza _____
12. chow mein _____
13. pierogi _____
14. braunschweiger _____
15. ricotta _____
16. sukiyaki _____
17. jambalaya _____
18. chicken tetrazzini _____
19. sauerbraten _____
20. pappadams _____
21. minestrone _____
22. shrimp curry _____

141

GA1309

CLOTHING

While many young people all over the world have become "Westernized" in the clothing they wear, traditional clothes are still popular and are even often preferred by some. This is especially true of older generations. The clothing we associate with a particular country or area is often the result of people dressing for the climate in which they live. Special hats and head-dresses, long flowing robes and thick padding are all good examples of people simply dressing for comfort.

There are also many styles of clothing that are worn for special reasons. Costumes designed for religious ceremonies and special celebrations are usually ostensibly distinctive and can be easily identified by others. Those who wear these "national costumes" wear them with a pride that will cause others to readily recognize them.

Choose a country of interest to you and research its native dress. Identify in descriptive terms the clothing of that culture. Use pictures from magazines or drawings to better describe the clothing. Identify whether the clothing is worn out of comfort to suit the climate or for a special ethnic or religious celebration.

Country:

Description of clothing:

Reason(s) for wear:

GA1309

BELIEFS AND RELIGIONS

People around the world belong to different religions and have different belief systems. Some primitive tribal people in Africa and South America have their own systems of worship and beliefs, but most of the world's people follow the teaching of one of the religions described below. After you have read and carefully studied each of the descriptions, identify the religion. Some you will already know and identify easily. Others may require some additional research.

1. _____ Its symbol is the cross. Those who follow this religion believe that a man called Jesus was sent to earth by God to bring peace. Jesus spent his life healing the sick and teaching people about God. He was crucified and followers believe he rose from the dead and ascended into Heaven. They believe that they, too, will go to Heaven when they die if they have lived good lives.

2. _____ Its symbol is the crescent shape of a new moon. The holy book is the Koran which the followers of this religion believe contains the words of God spoken to them by their prophet Muhammad. Their holy city is Mecca, and they worship in mosques. People of this religion take time out of their day five times daily to face toward Mecca and pray.

3. _____ It is the world's oldest religion. Those who follow this religion worship a Divine Being they call Shiva. They have shrines in their homes, and they believe in reincarnation. The Ganges River is sacred to them, and they hold animals in high esteem because they believe all living things have souls. They especially regard cows as sacred. They also honor the caste system, which is a social ladder that requires a person to associate with only those of his own caste—that caste being determined by birth.

GA1309

BELIEFS AND RELIGIONS

4. _____ The Star of David is the symbol of this religion which teaches that God gave Moses the Ten Commandments on how life should be lived on this earth. The most holy book of this religion is called the Torah, which is written by hand in the Hebrew language. The Sabbath is the holy day to all who follow this religion, and they begin its observance on Friday at sunset. The Sabbath ends when darkness falls on Saturday evening. Their place of worship is called a synagogue and their religious leader is the rabbi.

5. _____ People who worship this religion follow the teachings of a man called Gautama, who is known as the Buddha. He preached that people would be happy and have peace of mind if they led good lives and avoided being selfish. The state of everlasting peace was called Nirvana. To help them lead better lives, those who follow this religion visit shrines and the men spend part of their lives in monasteries. They shave their heads and spend much of their time in meditation.

6. _____ This religion was started by Guru Nanak, who believed that the caste system was wrong. His main belief was that people should worship only one god. The holy book is called the Granth and their leaders are gurus. Men and women are not allowed to cut their hair.

7. _____ This religion has its roots in ancient Japan. People today who follow this religion worship spirits at shrines where they have prayer notes and offer food and money.

In addition to these major world religions, there are people in primitive cultures who follow tribal beliefs of their own. Many were founded to drive away "evil spirits." Some involve witchcraft and a belief in magic. Others teach ancestral worship for the protection of the living. Special masks, herbs, beads, body paint and costumes are all a part of this tribal worship. In the past few years many people who followed the worship of these tribal religions have changed their faith to one of the more recognized religions.

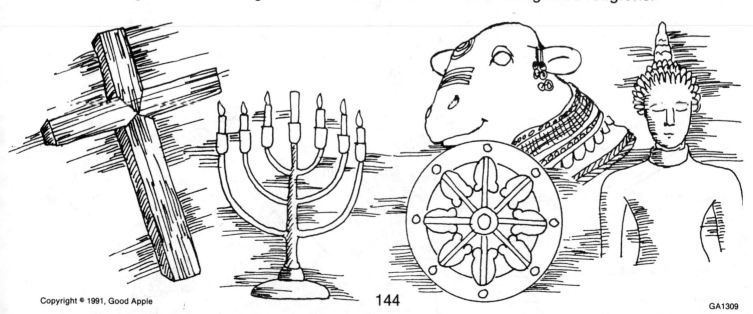

GA1309

MAPPING THE MAJOR RELIGIONS

On the outline map of the world below, draw in an area for each of the religions you've identified in this activity as being the predominate religion. Create your own key using whatever colors or markings you choose. If you know of other areas in the world where their religions are dominant, include them on your map. Share your finished map with other members of your class.

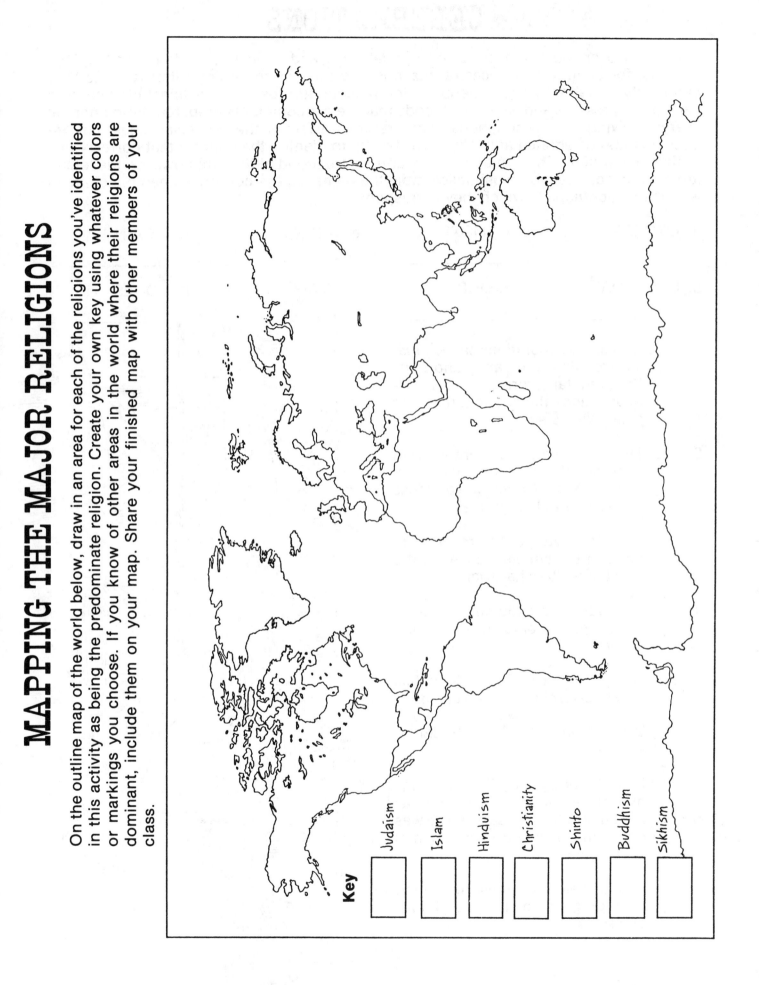

Key

Judaism

Islam

Hinduism

Christianity

Shinto

Buddhism

Sikhism

145

CELEBRATIONS

People all over the world celebrate special days and special occasions for religious reasons, for cultural and ancestral reasons and for just about any other reasons they can justify. Celebrations give people good reasons to dress in their finest clothes, give each other presents and eat special foods that are not commonly prepared during normal everyday living. The descriptions below refer to a few of these special times that are observed and celebrated annually. Your task is to identify the country that corresponds to that celebration. The names of the countries are found at the top; however, the letters are scrambled. First you must unscramble the names of the countries; then match them with the celebrations to which they correspond.

a. EGCEER _____

c. OEMCXI _____

e. AIDIN _____

g. HCAIN _____

b. LOLDNHA _____

d. AAJNP _____

f. LTAIY _____

h. TOIVES NOUIN _____

1. ____ Christmas decorations called *pinatas* are filled with candy and nuts. Children take turns being blindfolded and attempt to break the pinata with a stick.

2. ____ The New Year is celebrated with patterns of rice flour placed on doorsteps to welcome the goddess of wealth into their homes.

3. ____ On May Day soldiers parade through the streets displaying the latest in military hardware.

4. ____ It is tradition at weddings for guests to pin money onto the bride and groom.

5. ____ On December 6, Santa Claus fills the shoes of children with presents.

6. ____ For weddings, the bride traditionally wears a kimono.

7. ____ In this country Lady Befuna brings gifts on January 6 because she was too busy to find Jesus when he was born, and now she looks for him everywhere.

8. ____ People celebrate their new year, with dragons, dancing and firecrackers.

146

GA1309

HOMES

Another of life's necessities common among all peoples of the world is the need for shelter. The choice of building materials and the design and style of homes varies according to climate, environment, tradition and availability of materials. In the drawings and descriptions below and on the next page are examples of some of the many different kinds of homes in which people live. After looking carefully at each, decide on a place where you think such a structure would be a typical home. Jot down your answers and share your choices with other members of your class. Investigate other sources on homes around the world to validate your choices.

1. Large sheep ranches cover thousands of square kilometers. Ranch hands ride motorbikes and children must get their education via two-way radio and satellite television.

   Location: _____

2. These people must travel from place to place in search of water and pastures. They live in tents called *yurts* which are made of several layers of felt and are supported by a wooden frame. Each tent contains three areas: one for sleeping, one for the men and one for the women.

   Location: _____

HOMES

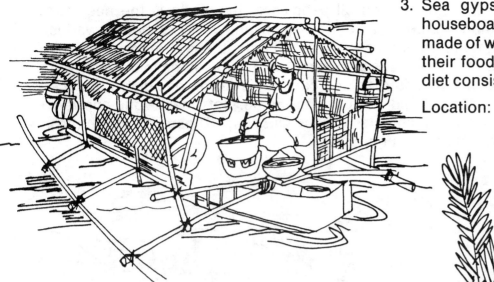

3. Sea gypsies live, eat and sleep on houseboats. The walls and roofs are made of woven rushes. The people cook their food in an earthenware pot. Their diet consists mainly of fish and cassava.

Location: _____

4. People in more primitive and remote areas sometimes live in caves high up in the rocks. They climb trees, swinging on vines to reach their homes, and live on wild plants, flowers, lizards and snakes.

Location: _____

5. People in high mountainous areas with heavy snowfall live in chalets. The ground floor is made of stone and serves as a stable in the winter. The rest of the house is made of wood with a gently sloping roof.

Location: _____

6. People in jungle climates sometimes live in palm-thatched houses located in areas that are cleared within the jungle. There are no windows and as many as twenty-five people may live in these huts together. They live by hunting and fishing.

Location: _____

GA1309

HOMES

7. In hot, dry countries, houses are made of mud and straw molded into bricks that become rock-hard when baked by the sun. The thick walls insulate the inside from the burning sun. They have low doorways and no doors. Often a family will own an entire cluster of the huts with each person having his own room.

Location: _____

8. In areas on the edges of deserts, people sometimes live in homes below the ground. They dig into the soft rock to a level of 15-25 feet (4.5-7.6 m). Here they find shelter from the heat and blowing sand as well as water. Several families often build their homes together and share a central courtyard.

Location: _____

9. In cold arctic lands life is sometimes difficult. Homes are built for survival and are often lined with fiberglass to ward off the cold. Some hunting is done when the weather permits, but there are periods when life outside is almost impossible.

Location: _____

. . . And in the Future

With our ever-growing population, scientists continue to explore the possibilities of people living elsewhere—namely under the sea and out in space. Research the current material available on these new horizons and speculate on what you feel are the implications of such living. What would be the pluses and minuses of this kind of life? Would you want to live there? Explain.

_____

_____

_____

_____

_____

GA1309

PEOPLE IN HIDING

The list below contains the names of thirty countries that dot the planet Earth. Hidden in the maze of letters below the list are the names of the people who live in those countries. For example, in the list you will find the *United States*. Knowing that people who live in the United States are called *Americans*, you would then be searching for the letters (forward, backward, horizontal or vertical) that together spell *Americans*. When you find them, circle those letters.

United States	Netherlands	Ireland	Scotland	Denmark
Burma	Cuba	Italy	Switzerland	Mexico
Poland	Laos	Sweden	Soviet Union	Wales
Australia	Canada	Kenya	China	Panama
Japan	Israel	France	Pakistan	Swaziland
United Kingdom	Finland	Spain	Iraq	India

```
I C A N A D I A N S I Q A R I A E V A L
N H C O S I D P A K I S T A N I S G S O
D I S S W C U B A N S A W O E R I H N A
I N N E I U T U E S E M R U B F L E A T
A E A D S D C H P O L E S O T R E S I I
N S Y E S R H S I T I R B S A E A E N A
S E N W C L O I E N F I N N S N R N A N
L F E S O O A R K H A C F A E C S A M S
F K K I T A L I A N S A K C N H I P A J
S T H I S R U S S I A N S I A T A A N I
E A U S T R A L I A N S T X D Y M J A L
N S P A N I A R D S H O W E L S H P P E
D S W A Z I S S N P I R A M A J O N S E
```

150

A PLANET IN PERIL

Few question the fact that the planet Earth is currently in its most dangerous state of environmental disrepair ever! The pollution of our waters, the deforestation of our land, the destruction of the ozone layer, acid rain and the garbage overload are the imprints of mankind. What we inherited from the damage done by those who came before us and what we are doing now to destroy our earth add up to all of our current problems. How we leave the planet for future generations depends on what we do now.

As bleak as the picture may seem, it is not too late to reverse the current problems. In the activities you have completed to this point, you no doubt became aware that there *are* things that can be done. In short—*you* can make a difference! In the pages that follow, questions will be asked that will help to reinforce the importance of your own actions. You will leave but one imprint of your life on the planet Earth, but that single imprint can contribute a great deal toward creating a livable environment to our benefactors.

151

GA1309

CREATE A BUTTON

One of the greatest hopes for cleaning up our environment lies in the education of the people who live on this planet. Recent television documentaries, Hollywood movies, statistics released by the Environmental Protection Agency, and news features, articles and editorials have all helped to bring about a public awareness that is working. Another avenue comes in the way of advertising. Billboards, spot radio ads and clever bumper stickers help to make the driver subconsciously aware of the need for action. Pin-on tags and buttons are yet another form of advertising that lets the world know of that person's support. Below are a few button ideas that get across the message of environmental education. Your task is to create one of your own in the blank in the middle. Make your message clever, yet meaningful. Make your button more attractive with the use of colored markers or crayons. Share your message with other members of your class. Create a class bulletin board that will show to all who visit your classroom how you feel.

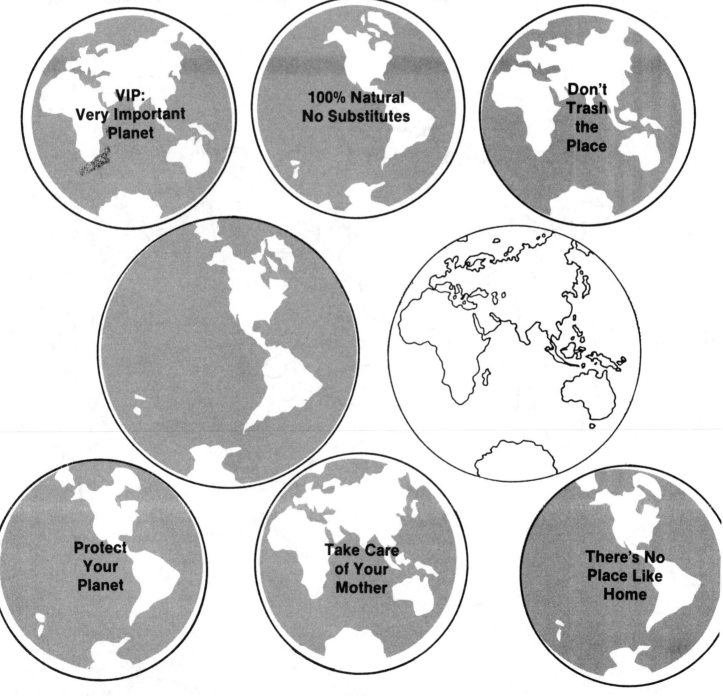

PRIVATE INVESTIGATIONS:
WHAT CAN I DO . . .

In the pages that follow you will be asked to investigate some of the ways in which you yourself can contribute toward the repair of our fragile planet. Finding out what to do, however, is the easy part. Putting your findings into practice is what really matters!

153

GA1309

... IN MY HOME?

While you are too young to own your own home, you can take a good look at some things that may be going on at your house that you can correct. You can also make observations to your parents that can help to make a difference. Consider the following.

1. Check for leaks around doors and windows. Use a lighted candle to see if there are energy leaks. A flame that moves is evidence that your home needs better weather stripping. Aside from saving your parents' money, what are the implications of such leaks on the environment?

   _____

   _____

   _____

2. Turn off the lights when not in use. While the benefits here are obvious, there are some additional steps you and your parents can take in lighting your home to save money and energy . . . and as a result, help to save the environment. Can you think of any?

   _____

   _____

   _____

3. Do you know about radon? It is an odorless gas that is found everywhere. When it becomes trapped in homes and a large concentration accumulates, it can be very dangerous for your health. It is estimated by the Environmental Protection Agency that as many as 10 percent of American homes have levels of radon that are too high. Investigate the source of radon and find out if your home has been tested. What can be done to reduce levels in homes found to have high levels of radon?

   _____

   _____

   _____

4. Take a close look at the furniture in your home. If you find mahogany or teak, you may marvel at its beauty, but you should realize at the same time that it came from a tropical forest. Every hour of every day 3000 acres of rain forests are destroyed. At the current rate, there will be no rain forests left one hundred years from now. What other substitution can you suggest to your parents the next time they buy a new piece of furniture?

   _____

   _____

   _____

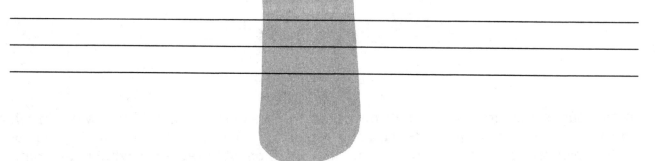

GA1309

5. What about the drinking water? In many areas of our planet, the drinking water has become contaminated and has been blamed for the cause of several health-related problems. Find out from your local water supplier how safe the water you drink and shower in really is. If there is a problem, what steps should you take to ensure that your family is consuming water that is safe? Is bottled water always a good answer?

_____

_____

_____

6. Saving water. It is estimated that 15-20 percent of our treated water is lost through leaking pipes and poorly fitted seals. There are also some steps we can take in the bathroom and the kitchen to dramatically cut the consumption of water. Talk about your ideas with your parents and jot down your summary below.

_____

_____

_____

7. Protecting the ozone layer. You learned earlier that chlorofluorocarbons are the villains that are damaging the ozone layer. Find out where they are in your home and how you can avoid their use.

_____

_____

_____

8. In addition, there are other things in your home that you may not have thought about before that are harmful to the environment. In the space that remains, list at least five other culprits that you currently use in your home that you can either eliminate altogether, find substitutes for or find different ways to destroy.

_____

_____

_____

...IN MY BACKYARD?

There are a number of things you and your family can do to your own lawn and garden to help restore the environment. The questions below should get your mind to thinking. Beyond that, it's up to you.

1. Perhaps you've heard that planting trees helps the environment. You probably already know that one of the big advantages of trees is the shade they provide. Studies have shown that trees can cool areas they shade by as much as 10^0-12^0. Trees also provide homes for birds and wildlife that are so much a part of our natural environment. What you may not know is how these "natural air-conditioners" can help to reduce global warming. Find out how and explain in the space below.

_____

_____

_____

_____

2. When it comes to lawn care, many people feel they must apply pesticides and herbicides to keep the pests away, the grass green and eliminate the weeds. Nothing could be further from the truth. There are chemical-free techniques that work equally effectively in maintaining a beautiful lawn without causing harm to the environment. Investigate these methods and describe briefly below.

_____

_____

_____

_____

3. The Mosquito Menace. None of us enjoys the itching caused by a mosquito bite. Millions of dollars are spent annually by people all over the world in a futile attempt to destroy, or at least repel, this flying menace. Not only are the sprays and chemicals used harmful to the environment, they are seldom effective for any length of time as the mosquito develops a quick immunity to them. There are, however, some steps you can take to combat the mosquito menace in your home and backyard. Research this subject and jot down your findings in the space below.

_____

_____

_____

_____

GA1309

...IN MY BACKYARD?

4. Organic gardening is much more than simply avoiding the use of insecticides. It involves a number of steps that will rebuild the soil as well as create a desirable environment for insects and birds that will allow for continued growth year after year. The real secret to organic gardening lies in properly feeding the soil. And the secret to feeding the soil lies in feeding the bacteria that dissolve the dead animal and plant nutrients that will in turn restore the soil by feeding the new plants the nutrients they need. Find out how you can naturally accomplish feeding the bacteria the way synthetic fertilizers do and report your findings below.

_____

_____

_____

_____

5. As stated earlier, composting is the most effective way to rebuild the soil in your garden. Composting is really nothing more than reducing organic wastes to humus. Investigate how you can create a compost in your own yard and jot down the steps involved in the space that remains. Choose a spot that is level and easy to collect your materials.

_____

_____

_____

_____

GA1309

... AT THE GROCERY STORE?

1. Do you realize that each of us throws away packaging containers equal to our own weight approximately every thirty days? This startling statistic helps to account for the global nightmare of disposing of our garbage. While America ranks high on the list, many other countries around the world are also faced with the problem of shrinking landfill space. Toxic contamination, caused by certain plastics used to make food containers, and acid rain—the result of their manufacture—place additional stress on our earth and environment.

Think about the problems associated with packaging food products, and then think about how those packages and containers affect our environment. Look at the list below and decide the following:

What kind of container is currently being used to package the item?

Can that container be reused or recycled (yes)?

Or is the container difficult to dispose of (no)?

For those which cause harm to the environment because of their disposal difficulties, offer a suggestion for each on alternative packaging.

Item	Container in Use	Reused/Recycled (Yes) Disposal Difficulties (No)	Alternative Packaging
Soft drinks			
Milk			
Potato chips			
Toothpaste			
Cereal			
Canned corn			
Bread			
Frozen corn			
Fresh fruit			
Taco sauce			
Catsup			
Hair spray			

... AT THE GROCERY STORE?

2. We are constantly bombarded with results of testing that prove the statement that eating less meat would improve our diets and help us to live longer. Let's think about some other benefits. How could eating less meat help our environment?

_____

_____

_____

_____

3. Buying "organic" foods is not only good for your health. It is good for the environment. Find out the difference between organic foods and those not considered organic and point to how organic foods are less harmful to the environment.

_____

_____

_____

_____

4. What other ideas can you think of that could happen in the grocery store that could lead to a better environment?

_____

_____

_____

_____

GA1309

...IN MY COMMUNITY?

1. Many cities are taking steps to reduce their garbage problems by enacting legislation that will encourage people to join the campaign to recycle. Seattle, Washington, residents get their trash picked up free of charge *if* they place their cans, bottles and newspapers in separate containers. If they don't, they pay a hefty monthly pick-up fee. Over half of Seattle's households participate in the program. They're saving money and helping the environment at the same time. Brainstorm any other ideas you either know of or can dream up that would offer residents incentives for recycling or penalties for failing to participate.

_____

_____

_____

_____

2. When you throw away an old paint can or empty pesticide can, there is a good chance that can will wind up in a landfill where it may eventually leak into the groundwater. Such toxic wastes are dangerous and harmful to the environment. Even if your family is making a conscious effort to clean up the environment, there are, no doubt, at least a few containers in your home that contain hazardous wastes. How can you dispose of such containers when their contents are eventually consumed? How can you get others in your community not to throw their containers of such waste into trash bags?

_____

_____

_____

_____

GA1309

3. Many of our planet's major cities are now making a concerted effort to clean up the air that has been blamed for severe health problems to people and tarnishes the quality of life for all living things. Encouraging car pools, providing better public transportation and enacting laws that force people to behave certain ways have all helped. But there are also a lot of other things that can and are being done to improve the air around cities. In the space below, jot down some of the suggestions you have that will add to the list of community involvement in cleaning the air. Share your ideas with members of your class.

_____

_____

_____

_____

4. An idea for the birds . . . We all know that planting trees adds to the beauty of a community and provides a cooling effect in the summer. Trees also absorb a great deal of carbon dioxide from the air and provide homes for desirable birds. We can and should all support tree planting in our own communities. But what about the birds elsewhere? Here's some real food for thought. How could buying a hamburger at a local fast-food restaurant possibly contribute to the threat of losing a tropical bird on the list of endangered species?

_____

_____

_____

...IN MY SCHOOL?

Cleaning up our environment starts with education, and for this reason, most schools are already involved with environmental education. The EPA has probably been to your school with suggestions to test for radon contamination, problems associated with having asbestos and unpure drinking water. Hopefully all of these potential school hazards have already been dealt with in your school. Step one would be for you to find out.

Beyond that, however, there are other things you and the members of your class can do to ensure a better planet for the future.

1. Let's start in the cafeteria. Do you bring your lunch to school? If so, take a look at its contents and the container you used to transport it from home to school. If you eat in the school cafeteria, look at how the food is served. Do they use throwaway tableware or glass, silverware and reusable plastic? What about the food itself? How are the foods served, and is the manner in which they are being served helpful or harmful to the environment?

_____

_____

_____

_____

_____

_____

2. Did you know U.S. schools spend an average of $42 every year on every child in every classroom on energy alone? That averages out to about $1000 per classroom! With that in mind, there are some obvious savings that could take place. Grab a notebook and take a walking tour of your school, noting signs you recognize where your school could save money. Then organize your thoughts into a few well-chosen words for the lines below.

_____

_____

_____

_____

_____

LET'S SAVE OUR PLANET POSTER

Each student should be given a piece of white construction paper or poster board that measures approximately 18″ x 24″ (45 cm x 60 cm). The theme of the poster is "Let's Save Our Planet." The assignment is for each student to place himself in the role of the protector. What can each of us do to add a personal contribution toward restoring a healthier planet Earth? Students can use pictures cut from magazines or newspapers, or students may create their own original drawings with colored markers or crayons.

Each poster should depict an idea which the student feels he or she can participate in to help save the planet. Students may review their work from "Private Investigations" to brainstorm ideas!

When posters are complete, students share them with other members of the class. Finished posters then either become a class bulletin board or are posted in the halls and other locations in the school to promote a "Let's Save Our Planet" all-school campaign.

GA1309

PLANET EARTH: NOW HEAR THIS!

Imagine yourself an alien from a distant planet. You have come to the planet Earth to "take a look around." Possessing an intelligence that allows you to see into the future, you see a gloomy tomorrow for Earthlings. What the present generations are doing to the planet will diminish the quality of life for future Earthlings. But there is still time. You must convince them to alter their life-styles and change their habits immediately to protect the planet for the future. What advice do you leave before you return to your own planet?

_____

_____

_____

_____

_____

_____

_____

_____

_____

_____

_____

_____

_____

_____

_____

_____

_____

_____

_____

A FINAL NOTE

By now you should be very aware that the future of this planet depends upon the choices made by all of us right now and in the future. It is very clear that an environmental crisis is at hand. Unless we alter the current course of human activity, the future of our earth will be a less than satisfying environment. Listed below are some of the major concerns. You should now be aware of courses of action that will help to solve the current problems. In the space beside each, jot down your choices for the actions that will improve each situation.

Problem   **Solution**

1. Destruction of Rain Forests

2. Destruction of Wildlife

3. Destruction of the Ozone Layer

4. Erosion

5. Desertification

6. Greenhouse Effect

GA1309

A FINAL NOTE

7. Depletion of Natural Resources

_____

_____

_____

_____

8. Pollution of Air and Water

_____

_____

_____

_____

9. There are some who say that even if we actively engage in all these actions, there won't be enough to reverse the damage that has been done. Those who support this position feel that only drastic and immediate changes in life-style will restore the earth. This position is known as the Green Movement. To implement their policies they direct much of their energy toward Green Politics—support of political candidates who place the environment and quality of life and the environment at the top of their list of priorities. One of the symbols of the Green Movement is the sunflower. Can you think of any reasons for its choice as a symbol for this noble society?

_____

_____

_____

_____

_____

_____

_____

_____

Write your own reaction to this final statement: _The natural world is like an interconnected web of life._

_____

_____

_____

_____

_____

_____

_____

GA1309

GOING BEYOND....

To those who want to become further involved in the movement to save the planet, a list is provided to put you in touch with several of the recognized national and international environmental organizations dedicated to that end. Write to your top choice or several. Get involved! There's still time!

GREENPEACE—Action group advocating nonviolent protests against those who threaten endangered species. Favorite projects are saving Antarctica, saving the whales and opposing the use of nuclear power.

U.S. address:
Greenpeace, 1611 Connecticut Avenue, N.W., Washington, D.C. 20009
Canadian address:
Greenpeace, 427 Bloor Street, West, Toronto, ONT M5S 1X7, Canada

SIERRA CLUB—Organization concerned with nature and its interrelationships with man.
Sierra Club, 730 Polk Street, San Francisco, CA 94109

WORLD WILDLIFE FUND (WWF)—Campaigns to protect wildlife all over the world. This organization uses education as its main vehicle of showing the world the importance of nature.

U.S. address:
World Wildlife Fund, 1250 24th Street, N.W., Washington, D.C. 20037
Canadian address:
World Wildlife Fund, 60 St. Clair Ave. E, Suite 201, Toronto, ONT M4T 1N5, Canada

FRIENDS OF THE EARTH (FOE)—Campaigns to protect wildlife, natural habitats and improve the environment at local, national and international levels.

U.S. address:
Friends of the Earth, 530 7th Street, S.E., Washington, D.C. 20003
Canadian address:
Friends of the Earth, 53 Queen Street, Room 16, Ottawa, ONT K1P 5CS, Canada

OXFAM—Campaigns to improve health and social conditions in poor countries as well as providing aid where it is most needed.

U.S. address:
Oxfam, 115 Broadway, Boston, MA 02116
Canadian address:
Oxfam, 251 Laurier Avenue, West, Suite 301, Ottawa, ONT KIP 5J6, Canada

NATIONAL GEOGRAPHIC SOCIETY—Produces films, videos, books, puzzles, maps and other educational resources that focus on all aspects of natural and global education.
National Geographic Society, Dept. 98, Washington, D.C. 20036

NATIONAL AUDUBON SOCIETY—Operates wildlife sanctuaries across the U.S. and provides a wide array of environmental educational services and materials.
National Audubon Society, 930 Third Avenue, New York, NY 10011

SMITHSONIAN INSTITUTION—Promotes environmental education through a wide variety of programs and materials.
Smithsonian Institution, 1000 Jefferson Drive, S.W., Washington, D.C. 20560

THE WILDERNESS SOCIETY—Promotes preservation of wildlife and natural habitats.
The Wilderness Society, 1400 Eye Street, N.W., Washington, D.C. 20005

RAIN FOREST ACTION NETWORK—Works to save the rain forests.
Rain Forest Action Network, 466 Green Street, Suite 300, San Francisco, CA 94133

GEOWORDS

Since much of the material presented in this book deals with knowing and understanding the terms and concepts of geography, it is suggested that time be spent on actual identification of word definitions. Students will gain a better understanding of the terms as the material in the book is presented. However, an occasional classroom "briefing" through the use of the card game Geowords will add further reinforcement to student understanding. To ensure the durability of the game cards and to make them easier to handle, it is suggested that they either be laminated or covered with Con-Tact paper before being cut apart. If you want each student to have a set of cards for personal reference, reproduce both sides of each page before laminating and cutting individual cards.

To play Geowords, the class can be divided into as many teams as desired. The order of play is determined by a roll of the dice with the teams having the highest number going first. The cards are shuffled and placed at random inside a box of any size as long as the students cannot see the individual cards. A student from the first team selects a card and reads whichever side of the card that is showing. If the definition side is showing, the student reads the definition, then has ten seconds to respond with an answer of the correct word that corresponds to the definition. If the word side of the card is showing, the student reads the word aloud and then must respond with an appropriate definition that matches the word. Players are not allowed to confer with other team members about an intended response. A correct answer results in a point for the player's team. Play then proceeds on to the next team. If a student responds incorrectly, his team is not awarded any points, and the same word becomes the responsibility of the player in line for a question on the next team to play.

The first team to score the number of points designated by the teacher is the winner. Word cards that are used are set aside and not placed back into the draw box. A variation of the game is to award greater point values for questions answered in later rounds. If this is done, the winning goal should be adjusted accordingly. The game can also be a useful tool for two children in a learning center. The same rules apply, but a quiet version involves the use of a generic gameboard, a marker for each player and as many questions as are needed to get the winner from *start* to *finish* on the gameboard.

GA1309

1. Many wind turbines clustered together in the same area to produce electricity	9. The remains of plants and animals that decomposed millions of years ago and are now used as a source of energy
2. A flat-topped elevation of land with steep sides—smaller than a plateau	10. Scientists who study the vibrations of the earth
3. Heat energy generated from within the earth	11. Tents that are called home by those who live in desert lands and are constantly on the move in search of water
4. Theory that all the continents were at one time connected to the same land mass	12. Phenomenon of atmosphere that traps infrared radiation, causing warming effect
5. Rows of mirrors that reflect sunlight to a receiver where it heats water to generate electricity	13. Huge mass of slow-moving ice
6. Sections of a plateau that are broken up through erosion	14. A tropical storm in the Atlantic Ocean that contains wind speeds of at least 74 miles (119 km) per hour
7. Energy that is created by the force of moving water	15. Compressed and recrystalized granulars of snow that become grainy ice from which glaciers are formed
8. Method used to measure the magnitude of earthquakes	16. A phenomenon that occurs when a planet or one of its shadows gets in the direct path of the sun, thus causing a shadow to be cast on another body

GA1309

FOSSIL FUELS	WIND FARMS
SEISMOLOGISTS	MESA
YURTS	GEOTHERMAL ENERGY
GREENHOUSE EFFECT	CONTINENTAL DRIFT
GLACIER	HELIOSTATS
HURRICANE	OUTLIERS
FIRN	HYDROELECTRICITY
ECLIPSE	RICHTER SCALE

GA1309

17. A phenomenon that occurs when the sun warms the earth, in turn warming the air, causing it to rise and form clouds	25. A floating chunk of glacier
18. Layers of soil that can be visibly seen in a cross-sectional sample of soil	26. The deep shadow of an eclipse
19. Large flatland area that stands above surrounding land	27. A moving air mass is forced to rise because an obstacle (like a mountain) lies in its path
20. The study of everything both living and nonliving in an environment	28. The partial shadow of an eclipse
21. A scientist who studies soil	29. An imaginary line around the earth halfway between the North and South Poles, from which all lines of latitude are measured
22. Clouds that are layered or stratified and usually cover the entire sky	30. A tropical storm in the Bay of Bengal with wind speeds in excess of 74 miles (119 km) per hour
23. Deserts found near the tropic of Capricorn and the tropic of Cancer	31. Clouds that are characterized by curly or stringy formations that usually mean good weather
24. When the moon becomes positioned between the sun and earth causing a blockage of the sun's light striking the earth	32. Deserts that lie deeply into the interiors of major land masses

171

GA1309

	ICEBERG		CONVECTION
	UMBRA		HORIZONS
	OROGRAPHIC LIFTING		PLATEAU
	PENUMBRA		ECOLOGY
	EQUATOR		PEDOLOGIST
	CYCLONE		STRATUS
	CIRRUS		SUBTROPICAL DESERTS
	INTERIOR DESERTS		SOLAR ECLIPSE

172

33. The process by which marginal grasslands are transformed into deserts	41. The number of people who live in a defined area
34. Grasslands characterized by distinct seasonal changes that occur because of temperature changes	42. An animal that is on the hunt to find and feed on another animal
35. Clouds characterized by formations that appear heaped or piled one on top of another	43. When elevated to high concentration levels, this component of the earth's atmosphere could cause global warming.
36. The eventual wearing away of the land through the force of nature and the hand of man	44. The path of reusing materials in favor of wasting and replacing them
37. Soils that contain similar amounts of silt, sand and clay	45. A movement downward of minerals from one level of the soil horizon to another as a result of the downward movement of soil water
38. When the earth becomes positioned between the sun and moon—causing a blockage of light reflecting off the moon	46. A state of equilibrium among all living things and the environment
39. The line from which all lines of longitude are measured	47. A period of time when an animal hibernates or remains inactive
40. Vast bodies of water that cover over 70 percent of the earth's surface and are partially responsible for sustaining life on earth	48. The cutting down of trees to clear the land for farming or fuel

POPULATION		DESERTIFICATION	
PREDATOR		TEMPERATE GRASSLANDS	
CARBON DIOXIDE		CUMULUS	
RECYCLING		EROSION	
LEACHING		LOAMS	
BALANCE OF NATURE		LUNAR ECLIPSE	
DORMANT		PRIME MERIDIAN	
DEFORESTATION		OCEANS	

GA1309

49. Areas where trees grow close enough together to prevent a normal growth of vegetation at ground level	57. Imaginary lines that run horizontally around the earth . . . lines that are used to help pinpoint locations on the earth
50. A drawing that shows the interdependency of living things upon each other for food	58. Material that could harm or endanger that which lives if released into the environment
51. The scientific study of the ocean	59. The upper layer of the earth's atmosphere containing gas which serves as a screen from the sun's harmful ultraviolet rays
52. Lines of longitude, which converge at the poles, are often called _____.	60. A crack in the outermost layer of the earth's crust
53. Those areas of the earth that are dominated by grass as the natural vegetation	61. Grasslands characterized by warm temperatures year round accompanied by a rainy season and a dry season
54. A self-contained habitat and its community, including the interaction of all living things as well as their action on the nonliving elements	62. A coral reef in the ocean that looks like a low ring-shaped group of islets. A lagoon is found in the middle.
55. A seasonal change in the direction of the prevailing winds, causing alternating wet and dry seasons.	63. An area found in a desert that is fed by underground water sources
56. Deserts found on the leeward side of mountains	64. A violent rotating column of air, considered nature's most destructive storm

	LINES OF LATITUDE		FORESTS
	HAZARDOUS WASTES		FOOD WEB
	OZONE LAYER		OCEANOGRAPHY
	FAULT		MERIDIANS
	SAVANNAHS OR TROPICAL GRASSLANDS		GRASSLANDS
	ATOLL		ECOSYSTEM
	OASIS		MONSOON
	TORNADO		RAIN SHADOW DESERTS

GA1309

65. An area of land receiving less than ten inches (25.4 cm) of rainfall annually	73. The disappearance forever of a species from the earth
66. The flat, low-lying plain composed of clay, sand and silt that is found at the mouth of a river	74. A feeding pattern in which food passes from one living thing to sustain the life of another
67. A tropical storm in the western Pacific with wind speeds that exceed 74 miles (119 km) per hour	75. An animal that feeds on plants
68. Substances obtained from nature that can be used by man but cannot be replaced by him	76. A narrow passage of water that connects two larger bodies of water
69. An official count of the number of people who live in a defined area	77. The line of longitude from which all other meridians are measured
70. The means by which plants use the sun's energy to absorb carbon dioxide and release oxygen	78. Large natural streams of flowing water found on every continent
71. The process by which areas where trees were once removed are replanted	79. The sum total of all that defines the way of life of a group of people
72. Chlorine-based compounds that are blamed for the damage done to the ozone layer	80. A narrow strip of land that connects two large bodies of land

177

GA1309

EXTINCTION	DESERT
FOOD CHAIN	DELTA
HERBIVORE	TYPHOON
STRAIT	NATURAL RESOURCES
PRIME MERIDIAN	CENSUS
RIVERS	PHOTOSYNTHESIS
CULTURE	REFORESTATION
ISTHMUS	CHLOROFLUORO-CARBONS (CFC'S)

178

81. Deserts found near the ocean which have plenty of moisture in the form of fog but no rainfall	89. The contamination of an area with material that is unnatural to the environment
82. Organic material that is formed from the decay of plants and animals	90. A pesticide that is designed to control or kill insects
83. An outlier of land with a smaller cap than a mesa	91. Type of map that shows the boundary lines between countries
84. Condition when an area experiences a lack of precipitation over a long period of time	92. Low lying area on either side of a river
85. A specific area that is inhabited by plants and animals	93. Imaginary lines that run vertically around the earth converging at the poles
86. That ecosystem made up of the earth, its waters, the atmosphere and all of the living things contained therein	94. The mixture of gases that makes up the air that surrounds the planet Earth
87. An animal that feeds off other animals	95. A view of the world as a single interconnected system which cannot be realized and understood when studied as many separate parts
88. An animal that is being sought after by another animal	96. Momentary changes in the atmospheric conditions that are subject to change from one day to the next

	POLLUTION		COASTAL DESERTS
	INSECTICIDE		HUMUS
	POLITICAL MAP		BUTTE
	FLOODPLAIN		DROUGHT
	LINES OF LONGITUDE		HABITAT
	ATMOSPHERE		BIOSPHERE
	HOLISTIC VIEW		CARNIVORE
	WEATHER		PREY

180

97. A body of water that is completely surrounded by land	105. An animal that feeds on both plants and animals
98. The line where the earth and the sky appear to meet	106. The addition of water to a field to allow for the growth of crops that would, under normal circumstances, not grow there
99. Those necessities and luxuries that are essential to a certain level of living that is customary within a society	107. Index that measures the total goods and services that are generated within a country annually
100. Winds that blow from northeast to southwest in the Northern Hemisphere and from southeast to northwest in the Southern Hemisphere	108. The sum total of factors that affect an organism during its lifetime
101. The up and down motions of water	109. A set of organisms classified because of the similarities or ability to interbreed
102. Deserts that are so cold that the moisture is trapped in ice	110. Stretch of elevated land that determines the direction of the flow of rivers on opposite sides
103. Those who study population trends	111. An area of land that is completely surrounded by water
104. The process by which all living things adjust to their environment	112. Area with constantly warm temperatures throughout the year where there is no frost and rain falls nearly every day, annually totalling over 200 centimeters

181

GA1309

OMNIVORE	LAKE
IRRIGATION	HORIZON
GROSS NATIONAL PRODUCT	STANDARD OF LIVING
ENVIRONMENT	TRADE WINDS
SPECIES	WAVES
CONTINENTAL DIVIDE	POLAR DESERTS
ISLAND	DEMOGRAPHERS
TROPICAL RAIN FOREST	ADAPTATION

GA1309

113. The shape of the surface features of a geographic area	121. The swampy backwater of a river or lake, usually found in flat areas with poor drainage
114. Because lines of latitude never meet, they are often called ___.	122. The planet Earth's largest bodies of land
115. Marine ecosystems that consist of shallow enclosed areas where fresh water enters the ocean	123. The sum total of the weather conditions in a specific area over an extended period of time
116. A pesticide that is designed to kill or control plants	124. A narrow ocean inlet that reaches far inland, usually very deep because of glacial action thousands of years ago
117. Movement from an area that was once one's place of residence	125. Surface level of the ocean, used as the point of reference for measuring the altitude of the physical features on land
118. Type of map that shows the locations of the mountains, the highlands, lowlands and other physical features of a given area	126. A body of land that is almost completely surrounded by water
119. Waste disposal system whereby organic matter decays to become a usable product.	127. Molten rock found within the earth's crust and mantle . . . it is called lava when it reaches the earth's surface.
120. A term used by scientists to classify areas according to the plant and animal life within them	128. Air pollution that reduces visibility, most commonly found hovering over industrial cities

	BAYOU		TOPOGRAPHY
	CONTINENTS		PARALLELS
	CLIMATE		ESTUARIES
	FJORD		HERBICIDE
	SEA LEVEL		EMIGRATION
	PENINSULA		PHYSICAL FEATURES MAP
	MAGMA		COMPOST SYSTEM
	SMOG		BIOME

MAP SECTION

The following section contains these outline maps: the World, North America, South America, Asia, Africa, Europe, Australia, Antarctica. Also included are maps containing political boundaries for these continents: North America, South America, Europe, Asia, Africa.

Below are several suggestions on how to make good use of the maps.

1. Have students draw in the political boundaries on the outline maps. This will give them good practice in identifying proper locations of countries on the continents.
2. Have students locate all important physical features including mountain ranges, rivers, lakes, waterways, highlands and plains.
3. Have students locate areas on each continent where various products are manufactured in large quantities.
4. Have students locate areas on each continent where various natural resources are found in abundance and are exploited to the point of having an economic impact on that area.
5. Outline maps can also be used to plot historical events and can be designated for the following other uses: annual precipitation, class product maps, cultural maps, population distribution maps, natural vegetation maps, plus any other use the classroom teacher may choose.

The maps with political divisions drawn in can be used in many of the same ways as the outline maps, but in addition can be used by students to plot capitals and other major cities within each country.

GA1309

WORLD

NORTH AMERICA

GA1309

SOUTH AMERICA

188

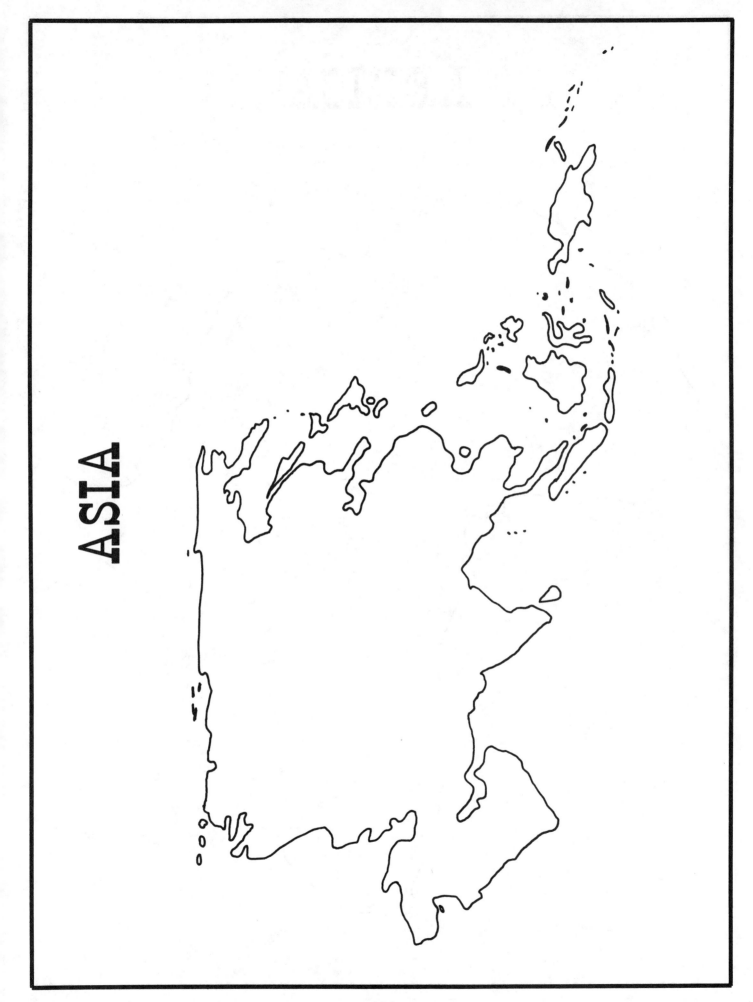

ASIA

189

GA1309

AFRICA

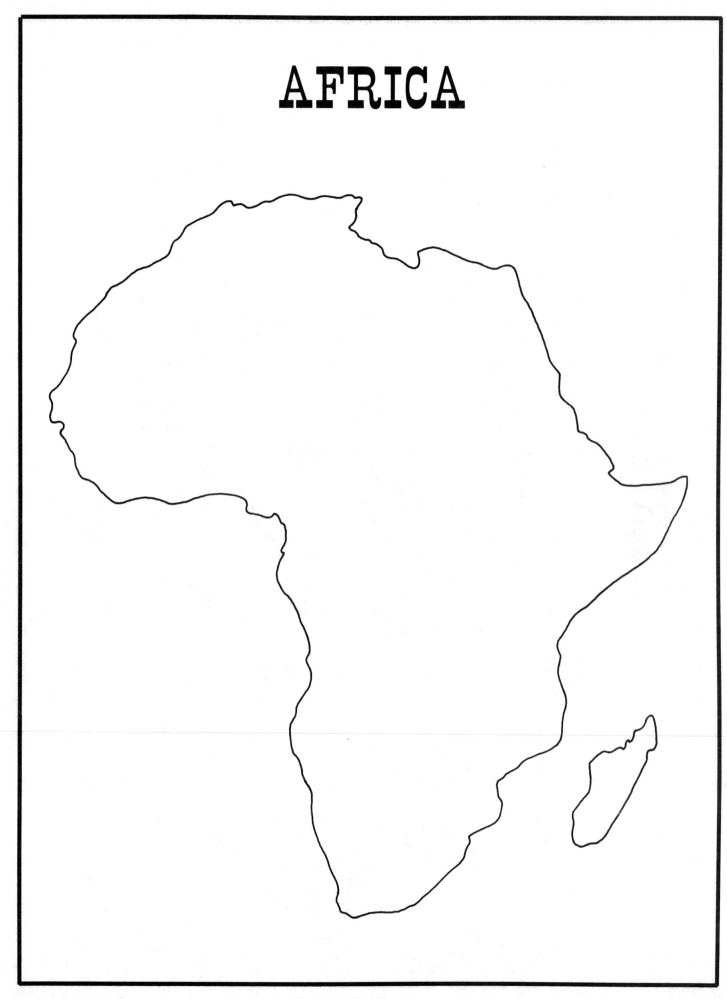

GA1309

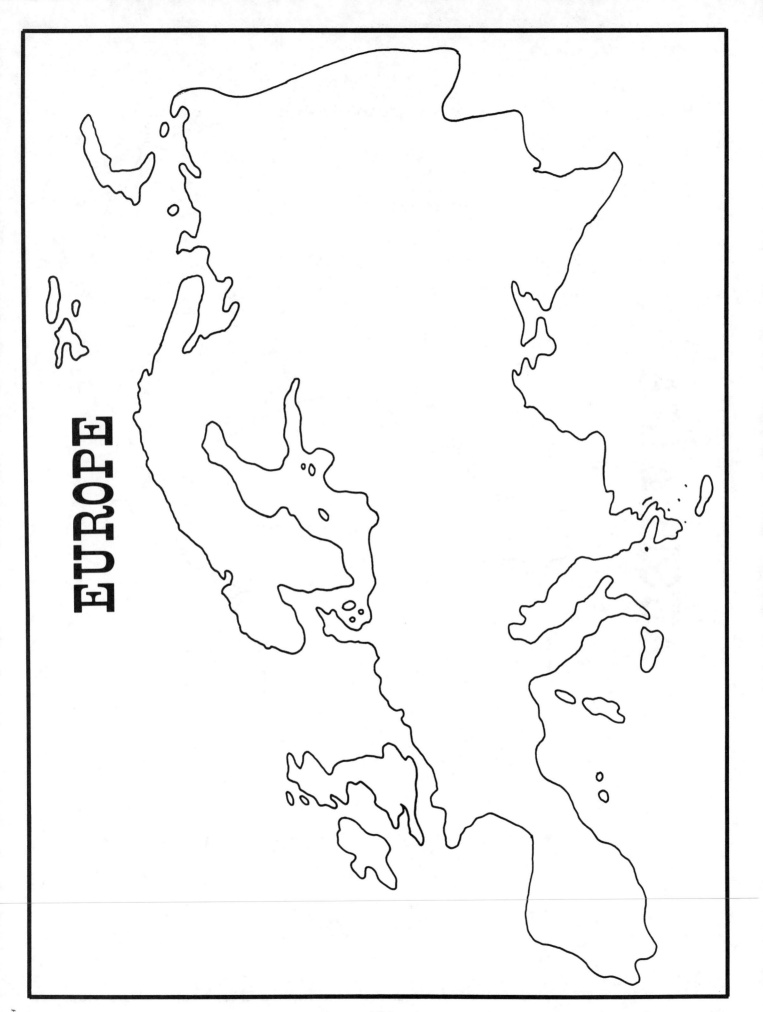

EUROPE

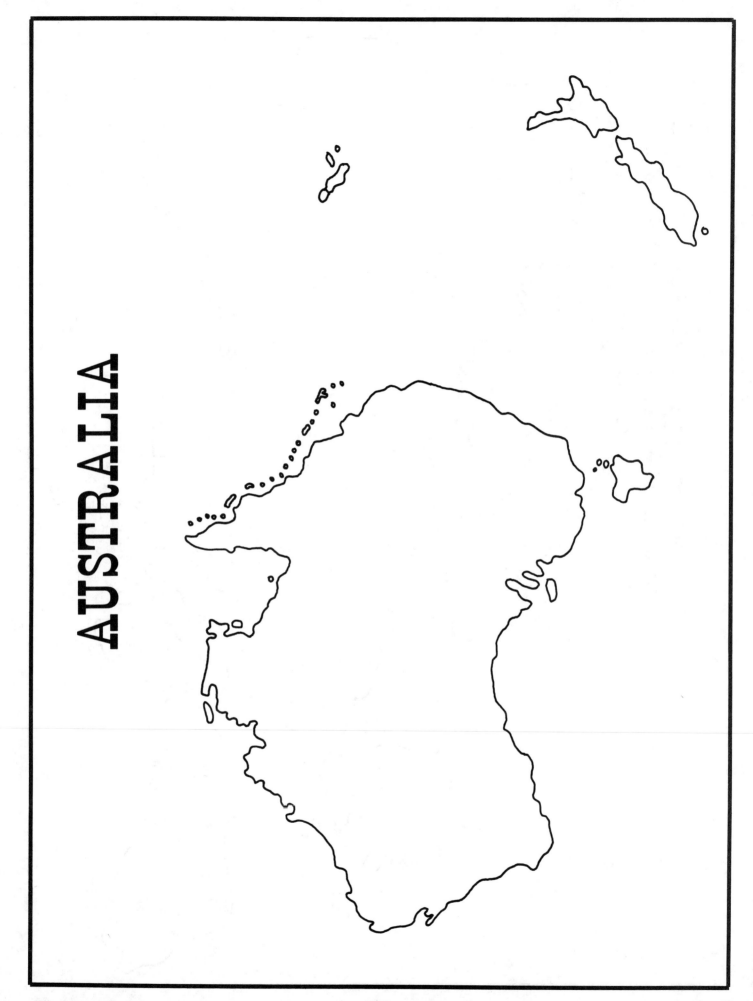

AUSTRALIA

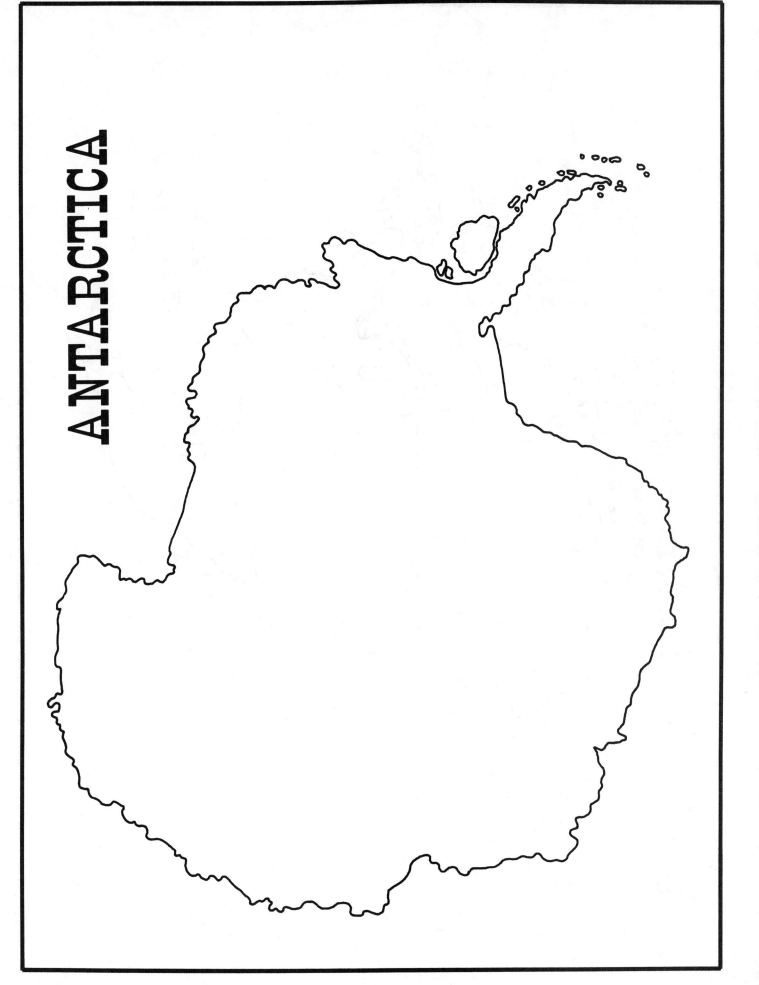

ANTARCTICA

GA1309

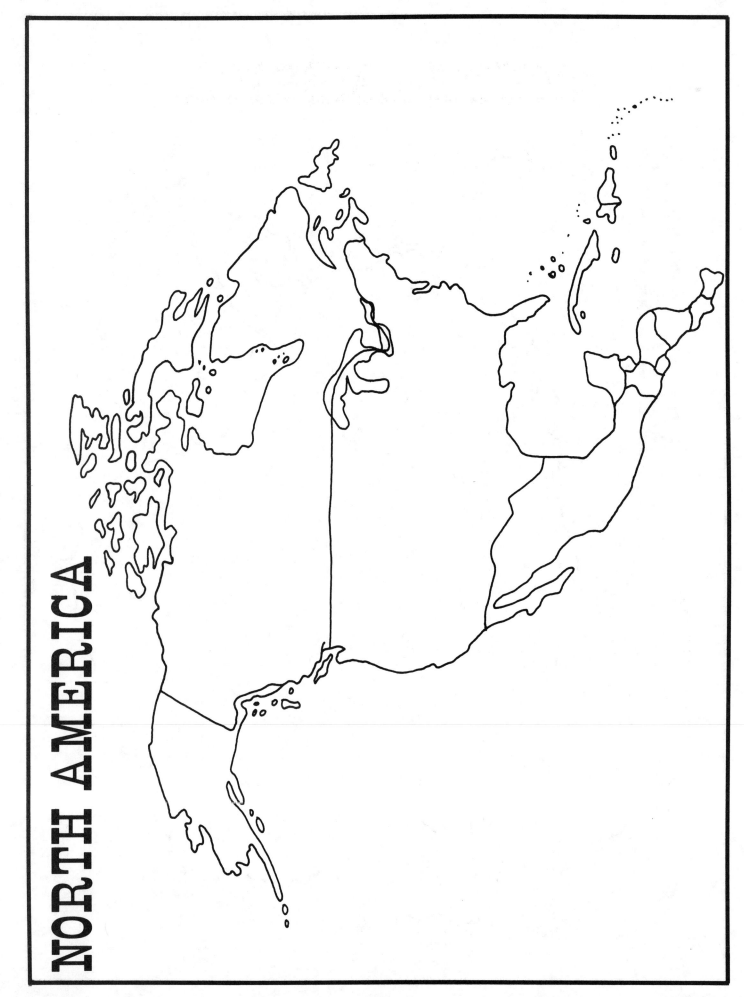

NORTH AMERICA

SOUTH AMERICA

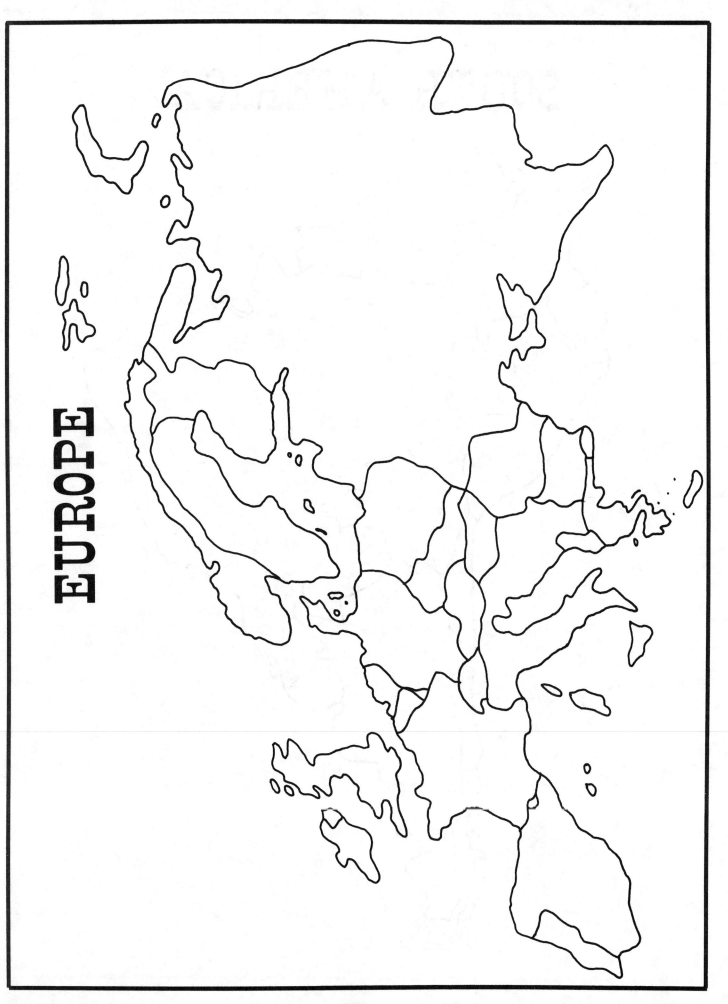

EUROPE

196

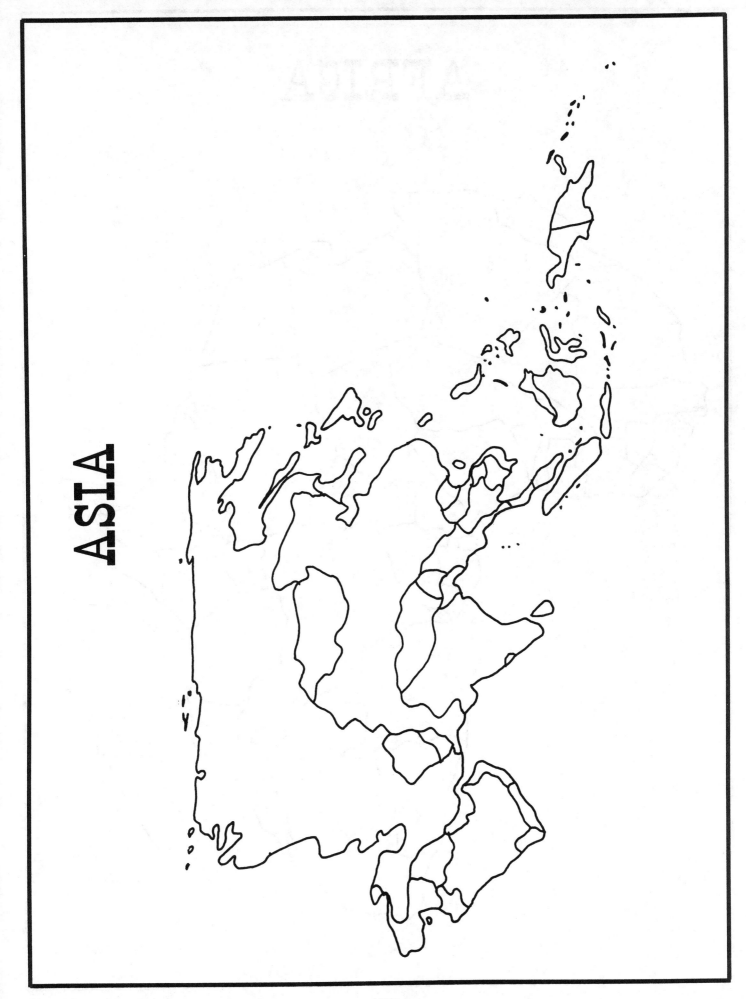

ASIA

197

GA1309

AFRICA

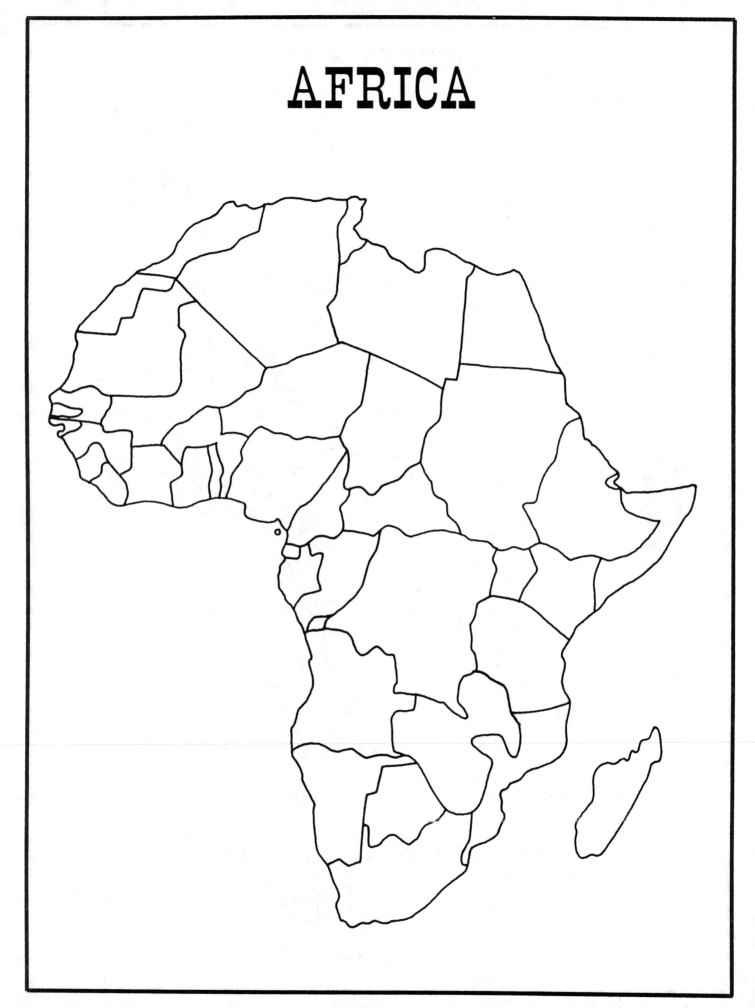

ANSWER KEY

Using Map Symbols Page 4
1. railroad
2. park
3. city or town
4. river
5. marina
6. road

Using a Compass Page 5
1. northeast
2. southeast
3. southwest
4. northwest

Which Way...USA? Page 8

1. SW	7. NE	13. S	19. W	25. SW
2. SW	8. SW	14. SW	20. NW	26. SE
3. E	9. NE	15. S	21. NE	27. SE
4. S	10. NE	16. SW	22. SW	28. W
5. SW	11. NW	17. SE	23. SW	29. SE
6. W	12. SW	18. NE	24. N	30. NW

View from the Top Page 10
1. south
2. east
3. west
4. southwest
5. Olympia
6. west
7. Los Angeles
8. Nairobi
9. southwest
10. east
11. northwest
12. Canberra
13. southeast
14. north
15. west

North Isn't Up! Page 11
1. east
2. south
3. west
4. west or northwest
5. south
6. north
7. southwest
8. northeast
9. west
10. north

Reading a Road Map Page 13
1. interstate
2. 10 miles
3. Interstate 21
4. southwest
5. 45 miles
6. Route B
7. east-west
8. Take Interstate 68 west to Morristown; then Interstate 21 south to Bernodotte.
9. 56 miles
10. Rock River
11. state highway
12. 73 miles
13. 27 miles
14. 38 miles
15. 72 miles

A Day at the Zoo Pages 14-15
1. east
2. northeast
3. east
4. north
5. southwest
6. northeast
7. eagles
8. southeast
9. no
10. west
11. south
12. southwest (accept west)
13. eagles and waterfowl
14. southeast
15. zebras
16. south
17. northwest
18. southwest
19. northeast
20. southwesterly

Midtown, Montana Page 17
1. C-3, B-3
2. F-4
3. D-5
4. A-1
5. B-7
6. C-3
7. F-2, F-3, G-1, G-2, G-3, H-1, H-2, H-3
8. B-5
9. G-6, H-6
10. E-2, F-1, F-2

Northern or Southern Hemisphere? Page 20

A = 20° N	F = 60° S	K = 30° N
B = 10° S	G = 40° S	L = 90° N
C = 40° N	H = 10° N	M = 5° S
D = 70° N	I = 0°	N = 35° N
E = 20° S	J = 30° S	O = 45° N

The Hemispheres Page 22
1. N and E
2. S and E
3. S and W
4. N and W
5. N and E
6. N and W
7. N and E
8. S and W
9. N and W
10. N and E
11. N and E

Pinpointing Major Cities Page 23
1. 55° N, 37° E
2. 40° N, 74° W
3. 36° N, 140° E
4. 22° S, 43° W
5. 19° N, 99° W
6. 51° N, 0°
7. 34° N, 118° W
8. 35° S, 149° E
9. 26° S, 28° E
10. 42° N, 12° E
11. 46° N, 77° W
12. 19° N, 73° E

Plotting the World's Major Cities Page 24
1. Berlin
2. Beijing
3. Chicago
4. Paris
5. Cape Town
6. Buenos Aires
7. Cairo
8. San Diego
9. Toronto
10. Wellington
11. Hong Kong
12. Caracas

Challenge Around the World Page 25
1. 25° N, 80° W, Miami
2. 22° N, 114° E, Hong Kong
3. 10° N, 66° W, Caracas
4. 38° N, 24° E, Athens
5. 44° N, 79° W, Toronto
6. 33° S, 151° E, Sydney

Measuring Distances with Latitude and Longitude Page 27
1. 69 miles
2. 65 miles
3. 60 miles
4. 53 miles
5. 45 miles
6. 35 miles
7. 24 miles
8. 12 miles

Distances Between Major Cities Page 28
1. 19° N, 99° W to 18° N, 72° E
   65 × 171 (99 + 72) = 11,115 miles
2. 41° N, 87° W to 40° N, 74° W
   53 × 13 (13 × 13) = 689 miles
3. 33° S, 18° E to 33° S, 70° W
   58 × 88 = 5104 miles
4. 43° N, 79° W to 44° N, 26° E
   49 × 105 = 5145 miles

Accept any answer that is reasonably close. Students may not be able to pinpoint precisely the locations of cities on the map provided.

Cities on the Same Longitude Page 30
1. 35° N, 139° E to 34° S, 138° E
   69 × 70 = 4830 miles
2. 30° N, 31° E to 15° N, 32° E
   15 × 70 = 1050 miles
3. 10° N, 66° W to 16° S, 68° W
   26 × 70 = 1820 miles
4. 40° N, 79° W to 25° N, 80° W
   15 × 70 = 1050 miles
5. 41° N, 87° W to 29° N, 90° W
   12 × 70 = 840 miles
6. 31° N, 121° E, to 14° N, 121° E
   17 × 70 = 1190 miles
7. 53° N, 6° W to 38° N, 80° W
   15 × 70 = 1050 miles
8. 42° N, 71° W to 18° N, 72° W
   24 × 70 = 1680 miles

Comparing Time Zones Page 32
1. 5 hours, 8:00 p.m.
2. 3 hours, 3:00 p.m.
3. 3 hours, 2:00 a.m.
4. 9 hours, 10:00 p.m.
5. 8 hours, 4:30 a.m.
6. 6 hours, 3:00 a.m.
7. 1 hour, 11:15 p.m.
8. 6 hours, 6:00 a.m.
9. 2 hours, 12 midnight
10. 1 hour, 10:15 p.m.
11. 7 hours, 2:00 p.m.
12. 8 hours, 4:00 p.m.
13. 7 hours, 1:30 a.m.
14. 5 hours, 12 midnight
15. 5 hours, 11:00 p.m.
16. 6 hours, 6:00 p.m.
17. 7 hours, 8:30 a.m.
18. 7 hours, 1:00 p.m.
19. 8 hours, 6:00 a.m.
20. 10 hours, 6:00 a.m.

Changing Times Pages 33-34
1. 4:04 p.m., Eastern Time
2. 9:49 a.m., Central Time
3. 11:17 a.m., Pacific Time
4. 2 hrs., 4 min., Mountain Time
5. 58 min., Pacific Time
6. 6:01 p.m., Eastern Time
7. 9:51 a.m., Mountain Time
8. 10:51 a.m., Central Time
9. 10:48 a.m., Pacific Time
10. 1 hr., 37 min.

Page 35
1. 2:00 p.m. EDT
2. 12 noon MDT
3. 11:00 a.m. PDT
4. 1:00 p.m. CDT
5. 2:00 p.m. EDT
6. 2:00 p.m. EDT
7. 2:00 p.m. EDT
8. 12:00 noon MDT
9. 11:00 a.m. PDT
10. 12:00 noon MDT
11. 1:00 p.m. CDT
12. 1:00 p.m. CDT
13. 1:00 p.m. CDT
14. 11:00 a.m. PDT
15. 12:00 noon MDT
16. 1:00 p.m. CDT
17. 2:00 p.m. EDT
18. 1:00 p.m. CDT
19. 1:00 p.m. CDT
20. 12:00 noon MDT
21. 2:00 p.m. EDT
22. 2:00 p.m. EDT
23. 11:00 a.m. PDT
24. 1:00 p.m. CDT
25. 11:00 a.m. PDT
26. 2:00 p.m. EDT
27. 11:00 a.m. PDT
28. 2:00 p.m. EDT
29. 2:00 p.m. EDT
30. 2:00 p.m. EDT

GA1309

International Date Line Page 36
1. 5:00 p.m., Saturday, July 3
2. 2:00 a.m., Sunday, July 4
3. 7:00 p.m., Saturday, July 3
4. 3:00 a.m., Friday, October 13
5. 6:00 p.m., Thursday, October 12
6. 11:00 a.m., Sunday, November 30
7. 5:00 p.m., Tuesday, June 1
8. 5:00 a.m., Friday, May 13
9. 10:00 p.m., Friday, November 11
10. 2:00 a.m., Thursday, January 5

Cloud Page 42
Cirrus: curly or stringy in shape. They usually are identified with good weather ahead.

Stratus: layered or stratified clouds that often cover the entire sky with a uniform cover

Cumulus: lumpy or heaped clouds. Their size determines the kind of weather they bring. The higher the clouds, the drier they are and the fairer the weather.

Page 43
Cumulonimbus: thunderhead clouds which occur along cold fronts but seldom produce rain

Cirrostratus: stratus clouds that are above 20,000 feet

Nimbostratus: clouds that produce a lot of precipitation

Stratocumulus: clouds that seldom bring rain

Stratus: clouds that may span the entire horizon and produce a light drizzle
1. cirrus
2. They almost always mean fair weather ahead.
3. nimbostratus
4. They are a sign of a lot of precipitation.

Continental Drift Page 48
1. Alfred Wegener
2. Pangaea
3. As the molten rock rises to the seafloor, it adds to the current seafloor and continents on either side of the fault are spread further apart.
4. The continents rest on a massive slab of rock made up of plates that form the earth's crust. As the plates shift, the surface of the earth is rearranged.

Latitude/Longitude Page 53
1. 69.4 miles
2. 1.16 miles
3. 102 feet

Rain Forests Page 55
2. Moisture absorbed by the trees evaporates through the leaves and returns to the earth as rain. The roots of the trees help to anchor the soil and prevent erosion. With the trees gone there is nothing to prevent rapid runoff.

Anatomy of a Rain Forest Page 56
Emergent layer: crowns of the tallest trees, torrential rains, scorching heat—harpy eagle, colobus monkey

Canopy: Leaves of middle-sized trees make a green canopy over the rest of the forest. Always shady and damp—gibbon, toucan, sloth, mandrill, chimpanzee, owl

Understory: vegetation stretches up seeking light, even cooler and wetter—leopard, python, tree frog, iguana, fruit bat, boa

Forest floor: dark and very damp, only small plants due to lack of sunlight—gorilla, wild pig, elephant, crocodile, tiger, snail, centipede, okapi

Underground: no light, root systems, animals that live in tunnels or burrows underground—armadillo, worm, mole, scorpion

Islands Page 57
Oceanic: formed by eruptions of volcanoes emerging from the floor of the ocean. Layers of lava build up until they eventually reach the water's surface.

Continental: Scientists believe that many years ago the land on earth was all connected as one huge continent. As breaks in the earth's crust caused the continents to break apart, some of the breaks caused large pieces to break off as islands.

Barrier: Ocean currents over a period of time can pile up sand along the coastlines away from the shore, eventually to the point where the deposited sand is above the water level.

Coral: islands that are formed out of the buildup of tiny coral polyps

Lakes Page 58
1. Caspian Sea: Buckling of the earth's crust created a deep crack which created the basin that was filled with salt water from the ocean.
   Great Lakes: Huge glaciers during the Ice Age gouged out huge basins that were later filled with fresh water.
   Lake Mead: Hoover Dam, built during the 1930's, holds back the Colorado River forming a huge reservoir.
2. Plant life and silt slowly begin to fill in the basin over a period of time. Eventually the bottom begins to fill in and becomes a swamp. As time goes on, the process continues until the lake eventually dries up.
3. water supply for cities, inland transportation, recreation, hydroelectric power and a source of food
4. Dumping sewage and chemical fertilizers destroys the oxygen and chokes off all that lives within the lake. Acid rain is another cause.

Eclipses Page 60
1. solar eclipse
2. lunar eclipse
3. lunar eclipse
4. umbra
5. penumbra
6. The moon is far enough from the earth that it doesn't cause any significant shadow on the earth.
7. They didn't understand the phenomenon, and solar eclipses were especially unsettling.

Grasslands Page 62
1. They break up passages for air in the soil and help to mix together the various soil components.
2. Overgrazing is caused when animals aren't allowed to roam freely. Once they are fenced in there is not enough vegetation to support the entire herd, so the animals graze the grass down to the roots.
3. practicing better methods of conservation, planting trees to hold the soil, avoiding overcultivation and recognizing our grasslands as a valuable ecosystem that should not be destroyed

Ecosystems Page 63
1. I
2. J
3. F
4. G
5. A
6. C
7. H
8. B
9. D
10. E

Erosion Page 65
2. Floodwaters often deposit tons of rich topsoil on the deltas, causing a problem where the soil was washed away but being a plus to the lands where the topsoil is deposited.
3. planting trees to hold topsoil, contour plowing, not over-grazing or overcultivating the land and allowing endangered areas to lie fallow to aid in their restoration

Richter Scale Page 66
1. 30 times
2. 900 times
3. 27,000 times
4. 13,500 times
5. to give seismologists a way of comparing various earthquakes historically and to give the general public a barometer of comparing the magnitude and predicted damage caused by larger earthquakes

Mountains Page 70
1. b, c, d, a
2. The sun's energy comes to earth by way of shortwave radiation. It is easily absorbed by the air near the earth, because there is more air to absorb that energy than there is high up on the mountain where the air is thinner.

Hurricanes Page 72
2. hurricanes, cyclones, typhoons
3. Hurricanes are tracked by sophisticated satellites, radar and weather planes. The center has a good idea where the hurricanes will come ashore and people are evacuated.

GA1309

Deep-Sea Data Page 77

1. Prevailing winds blow the water at the surface level. The winds also blow across the land. The ocean currents these winds cause do not pile up against the land. As a result, currents develop that flow in the opposite direction.
2. There are many minerals in seawater that have been washed into the sea from the land. As the sun causes much of the seawater to evaporate, the minerals remain and the water becomes even more concentrated with salt. In areas where there is a lot of fresh water, the water is not so salty. Where there is a lot of evaporation, the water is very salty.
3. As the wind pushes the water particles, they move around and around. As the waves approach the shore, the water becomes shallow and the depth of the seabed breaks up the smooth pattern of the rolling waves. The top of the wave breaks as it hits the beach.
4. The gravitational pull of the moon pulls the water on earth toward the moon causing a slight bulge or high tide. There are two high tides every twenty-five hours.
5. The ripples lie at right angles to the wind. The sand grains are blown up the gentle face and then fall down the steeper downwind face. As the power of the wave increases, the ripples are smoothed out.

Kinds of Desserts Pages 79–80

1. The warm air of the tropics near the equator rises. As this happens, it cools and drops heavy amounts of rainfall. The cooler, drier air then moves toward the tropic of Capricorn and the tropic of Cancer. The air then descends and warms. The resulting air is without moisture.
2. The warm air that blows off the land toward the water comes into contact with the cold water and produces fog but no rain.
3. The winds that reach this far into the interior simply have no moisture left.
4. There is indeed available water, but the temperature is so cold that it cannot rain.
5. As the air is forced up by the height of the mountains, the air cools and condenses into rain. By the time that same air moves over to the other side of the mountain, there is no moisture left.
6. overgrazing, overintensive farming, poor irrigation and change in climate

Kinds of Forests Page 84

1. C	4. D	7. C	10. C	13. C	16. D
2. D	5. D	8. D	11. D	14. C	17. C
3. C	6. C	9. C	12. D	15. C	18. C

Hiding in the Forest Page 85

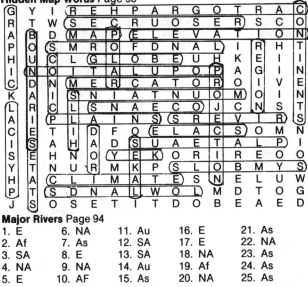

Minerals Page 87

Au: gold—bullion, jewelry, electronics
S: sulfur—sulfuric acid, sulfa drugs, plastics, rubber
Cu: copper—wiring, plumbing
Fe: iron—steel
C: diamond—jewelry, industry for cutting and drilling
U: uranium—fuel for nuclear energy
Ag: silver—jewelry, coins, electronics
Al: aluminum—frames, car parts, foil, food containers
NaCl: salt—preservatives, seasoning, road deicer
N: nickel—used in making steel, petroleum industry, coins
Hg: mercury—thermometers and batteries
SiO_2: quartz—prisms, lenses, time mechanism in clocks

Reading a Mineral Map Page 88

1. Nevada, South Dakota, Arizona, Utah, Oklahoma
2. Idaho, New York, Missouri, Colorado, Tennessee
3. Arizona and Utah
4. Texas, Louisiana, Kentucky, Tennessee, Idaho
5. California
6. Florida and North Carolina
7. Wisconsin and Minnesota
8. Texas
9. Minnesota and Michigan
10. Missouri, Colorado, Nevada, Utah

Mineral Dig Page 89

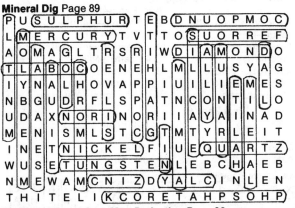

Maps and Equal Area Map Projection Page 90

1. The sizes and areas of the continents are correct.
2. The shape of Asia and parts of Europe are distorted.

Mercator's Cylinder and Conic Projection Page 91

1. Continents' shapes are not distorted nor are compass directions.
2. Greenland and land masses in higher latitudes are severely distorted.
3. Mid latitudes are accurately portrayed.
4. It is impossible to show the entire earth from this projection.

Polar and Interrupted Projection Page 92

1. It shows the shortest distance between any two points over the poles.
2. Land masses are distorted so the entire earth cannot be shown.
3. There is very little distortion of land masses.
4. It is impossible to show proper perspective of oceans.

Hidden Map Words Page 93

Major Rivers Page 94

1. E	6. NA	11. Au	16. E	21. As
2. Af	7. As	12. SA	17. E	22. NA
3. SA	8. E	13. SA	18. NA	23. As
4. NA	9. NA	14. Au	19. Af	24. As
5. E	10. AF	15. As	20. NA	25. As

GA1309

Rivers of the World Page 95

1. Mackenzie	10. Orinoco	19. Niger	27. Amur
2. Yukon	11. Amazon	20. Nile	28. Yellow
3. Missouri	12. Negro	21. Zaire	29. Ganges
4. Mississippi	13. Rio de la Plata	22. Zambezi	30. Indus
5. Colorado	14. Paraná	23. Volga	31. Brahmaputra
6. Rio Grande	15. Thames	24. Ob	32. Mekong
7. Ohio	16. Rhine	25. Irtysh	33. Yangtze
8. Tennessee	17. Rhône	26. Lena	34. Darling
9. St. Lawrence	18. Danube		

Great Rivers/Great Cities Page 96

1. d. London—Thames
2. g. Sydney—Parramatta
3. i. Seoul—Han
4. b. Washington, D.C.— Potomac
5. f. New York—Hudson
6. a. Calcutta—Hooghly
7. h. Delhi—Jumna
8. c. Paris—Seine
9. j. Vienna—Danube
10. e. Rome—Tiber
11. l. New Orleans—Mississippi
12. k. Cairo—Nile
13. m. Buenos Aires— Rio de la Plata
14. n. Shanghai—Yangtze

Anatomy of a River Page 97

1. source
2. lake
3. tributary
4. rapids
5. floodplain
6. marsh
7. delta
8. mouth

Hidden Rivers Page 98

The World's Largest Cities Page 100

a. 1, Indonesia
2, Brazil
3, Canada
5, Denmark
4, India

b. 4, Japan
2, Japan
1, China
5, West Germany
3, Chile

c. 4, United Kingdom
1, Mexico
3, U.S.A.
2, China
5, France

d. 1, India
3, India
5, Iraq
2, China
4, China

e. 4, West Germany
2, Turkey
3, U.S.A.
5, South Africa
1, Brazil

f. 4, U.S.A.
5, Italy
2, Iran
1, U.S.S.R.
3, Peru

g. 2, South Korea
4, China
5, Pakistan
3, India
1, Egypt

City Landmarks Page 104

1. E—Cathedral of St. Basil
2. C—Sydney Opera House
3. F—CN Tower
4. J—Great Sphinx
5. H—Taj Mahal
6. A—Eiffel Tower
7. D—Statue of Liberty
8. G—Parthenon
9. I—Leaning Tower of Pisa
10. K—Sears Tower
11. B—Palace of Westminster

Page 105

1. Statue of Liberty
2. Eiffel Tower
3. CN Tower
4. Leaning Tower of Pisa
5. Great Sphinx
6. Palace of Westminster
7. Taj Mahal
8. Sydney Opera House
9. Parthenon
10. Cathedral of St. Basil
11. Sears Tower

The World's Largest Outdoor Lab Pages 109-110

1. Norwegian explorer Roald Amundsen arrived at the South Pole in 1912 just thirty-four days ahead of British explorer Robert Falcon Scott. Scott was bitterly disappointed to have not been the first to arrive.
2. At stake is concern over the vast mineral wealth that lies beneath Antarctica. Some nations want to allow for the exploitations of minerals if done in a controlled manner that would not damage the land or environment, while other nations want a ban on mineral activity altogether. Those nations favor a movement to turn the entire continent into a world park.
3. Man-made gases called chlorofluorocarbons are trapped over Antarctica by winter winds. They react with sunlight to release chlorine atoms that destroy the ozone and allow harmful ultraviolet radiation. The "hole" in the atmosphere in Antarctica shows evidence that the same process may be occurring elsewhere.
4. chin strap penguins, blue whales, Weddell seals, Adélie penguins, Cape pigeons, gentoo penguins, minke whales, petrels, krill, phytoplankton, moose, Deschampsia and many species of fish
5. professionally led expeditions and ski trips
6. Disposal of waste is the big problem plus the fact that the more popular Antarctica becomes, the greater the eventual danger to the environment.
7. The organization is against any exploitation whatsoever. They would prefer that it become a world park, preserved forever in its natural state.
8. Answers will vary.

Soil Page 115

C, B, A, B

Erosion and Conservation Page 116

1. Planting smaller fields, providing windbreaks and planting shrubs and trees can help to reduce the effects of these poor farming techniques.
2. Planting different crops that will add nutrients that were taken from the soil by the plants of the recent harvest
3. Planting ground cover and replanting trees and shrubs to beautify the new landscape will also help to prevent further loss of topsoil.

Changing Climates Page 118

El Niño: A reverse in the direction of the trade winds every few years causes warmer water in the eastern Pacific and severe drought in southern Asia and Australia.

Sunspots: During periods when there is little sunspot activity, the earth became colder (16th century) because less sunlight was reaching the earth.

Greenhouse Effect: an accumulation of gases caused by the excessive burning of fossil fuels has destroyed part of the earth's ozone layer allowing the temperature to rise.

1. The ice caps could meet and cause flooding in coastal areas and drought in other places.
2. Answers will vary.
3. We can reduce the use of fossil fuels and reduce the level of chlorofluorocarbons.
4. The sun heats the earth, and the air around the earth absorbs the radiated heat. There is less air to absorb the heat at higher altitudes, so it is colder.

Our Major Climates Page 119

1. e
2. b
3. d
4. a
5. f
6. c

Climates Around the World Page 120

1. desert
2. continental
3. equatorial
4. desert
5. polar
6. equatorial
7. Mediterranean
8. desert
9. tropical
10. tropical
11. mountainous
12. Mediterranean
13. equatorial
14. continental
15. tropical
16. Mediterranean
17. continental
18. continental
19. continental
20. desert

GA1309

Comparing Continents Page 125
Asia: 108⁰, 30%
Africa: 76⁰, 21%
North America: 58⁰, 16%
South America: 43⁰, 12%
Antarctica: 32⁰, 9%
Europe: 25⁰, 7%
Australia: 18⁰, 5%

Page 126
Asia: 217⁰
Europe: 49⁰
Africa: 43⁰
North America: 29⁰
South America: 20⁰
Australia: 2⁰
Antarctica: 0⁰

Asia: 3,025,000,000
Europe: 675,000,000
Africa: 600,000,000
North America: 400,484,000
South America: 275,000,000
Australia: 25,000,000
Antarctica: 0

The Population of Asia Page 127
1. India, China, Bangladesh, Indonesia, Japan (accept any other highly populated countries in Asia)
2. High birthrate is the main reason.
3. Those areas with few people are mountainous and have more difficult living conditions.

A Slice of Energy Page 129
1. Crude Oil: 129⁰
   Coal: 96⁰
   Natural Gas: 68⁰
   Hydroelectricity: 28⁰
   Biomass: 20⁰
   Nuclear Energy: 18⁰
   Other: 1⁰
2. Crude Oil: 36%
   Coal: 27%
   Natural Gas: 19%
   Hydroelectricity: 7%
   Biomass: 6%
   Nuclear Energy: 5%
   Other: 0%
3. Answers will vary.

"Wave" of the Future Page 130
1. Answers will vary, but it could become a viable source of energy for areas currently without an adequate energy source. It also is renewable, another benefit that could make it a replacement resource for some of the fossil fuels we are currently using.
2. Corn is converted with ethanol—which is then blended with gasoline to create gasohol, a fuel that will power autos, trucks, etc. The advantage is that it saves on the use of gasoline, a fossil fuel that is nonrenewable.
3. Answers will vary.
4. Answers will vary.

Searching for Nature's Treasures Page 131

1. Europe
2. South America
3. South America
4. Asia
5. Asia
6. North America
7. Europe
8. Africa
9. Europe
10. Africa
11. Africa
12. North America
13. Antarctica
14. North America
15. Europe
16. Australia
17. Africa
18. North America
19. Asia
20. Europe
21. South America
22. Europe
23. Africa
24. North America
25. North America
26. Asia
27. Europe
28. Australia
29. North America
30. Europe

Nature's Wonders Pages 133-134
1. Victoria Falls, Africa
2. Grand Canyon, North America
3. Ross Ice Shelf, Antarctica
4. Baykal, Asia
5. Mount Fuji, Asia
6. Great Barrier Reef, Australia
7. Angel Falls, South America
8. Vatnajökull, Europe
9. Eisriesenwelt, Europe
10. Sugarloaf Mountain, South America
11. Old Man of Hoy, Europe
12. Badlands, North America
13. Big Sur, North America
14. Matterhorn, Europe
15. Kilimanjaro, Africa
16. Mount Everest, Asia
17. Cape Horn, South America
18. Amazon River, South America
19. Nile River, Africa
20. Aconcagua, South America

Language Page 137
1. t
2. r/t
3. g
4. l
5. c
6. i
7. d
8. e
9. k
10. c
11. b
12. f
13. c
14. k
15. k
16. g
17. h
18. m/g
19. n/q
20. k/o
21. s/r
22. p
23. k/r
24. a/k
25. j

Money Page 139
1. l, bolivar
2. k, ruble
3. h, dollar
4. g, peso
5. d, yuan
6. j, guilder
7. f, mark
8. b, lira
9. e, yen
10. a, dinar
11. i, franc
12. c, balboa

Money Changers Page 140
1. $81.50
2. 114.94 marks
3. 123,900 yen
4. 9.259 rupees
5. $.096
6. 157,272 lira
7. 9142.85 rubles
8. 94.68 rands
9. $1292.50
10. 152.51 yuan

Ethnic Flavor Page 141
1. France
2. Russia
3. Germany
4. Italy
5. China
6. Japan
7. France
8. Mexico/Spain
9. Italy
10. Germany
11. Italy
12. China
13. Poland
14. Germany
15. Italy
16. Japan
17. French in Louisiana
18. Italy
19. Germany
20. India
21. Italy
22. Malaysia

Beliefs and Religions Pages 143-144
1. Christianity
2. Islam
3. Hinduism
4. Judaism
5. Buddhism
6. Sikhism
7. Shinto

Celebrations Page 146
1. c, Mexico
2. e, India
3. h, Soviet Union
4. a, Greece
5. b, Holland
6. d, Japan
7. f, Italy
8. g, China

Homes Pages 147-149
Examples:
1. Australian outback
2. Arabian Desert
3. islands near Southeast Asia
4. remote areas in Philippines
5. Switzerland
6. jungles of Borneo
7. South America
8. Sahara Desert
9. near Arctic Circle

People in Hiding Page 150

203

GA1309

. . . In My Home? Pages 154-155

1. waste of precious energy plus the air pollution and acid rain caused by the wastes of creating the energy
2. using fluorescent bulb lighting, dimmer switches, frosted bulbs, reflector bulbs and the new energy-saving light bulbs
3. The source is usually uranium in the soil on which homes are built. Sealing cracks in basement floors, installing basement ventilation systems and getting professional help are methods of reducing the levels of radon.
4. Cherry, birch, maple, oak and pine are all replaceable woods that make attractive furniture and do not contribute to deforestation.
5. Contact the EPA. Have water tested, flush pipes, install filters and use bottled water. No, it's not always safe.
6. Answers may vary but should include turning off the tap when possible, buying efficient dishwashers, toilet dams, water-saving shower heads and flow-control faucets.
7. Refrigerators use a refrigerant in the cooling unit. Some aerosol sprays contain CFC's and Halon fire extinguishers. Avoid buying such products and since all refrigerators have them now, make sure the cooling unit does not leak and that it is destroyed properly when it wears out.

. . . In My Backyard? Pages 156-157

1. Trees use carbon dioxide which gets into our atmosphere through the burning of fossil fuels. An overabundance of CO_2 in our atmosphere has trapped the sun's rays before they can bounce back away from the earth. The result is that the earth becomes warmer. Trees absrob some of this CO_2, thus reducing the level.
2. Mow only when needed; water properly; use toxic-free chemcial controls; leave clippings to decompose and provide natural fertilizer; feed soil with nitrogen, potassium, calcium, sulfur and bonemeal.
3. Eliminate containers that allow for standing water. Repair holes in screens and cracks where they may get into your house. Do outside chores at times when mosquito activity is lowest (midday). Apply repellent to your clothing rather than skin. Wear a long-sleeved shirt and a hat. Look for sources where mosquitoes are often found.
4. Compost is the easiest way, but you can also make your own fertilizer using bonemeal, kelp, green sand, rock phosphate, peat moss, humus and decomposed leaves. Soil can also be tested to let you know which you are lacking and which you do not need.
5. Choose a spot that is level and easy to collect your material. Build a compost bin of wire or concrete blocks to contain material. Create layer after layer of sticks, wood chips, grass clippings and garden soil. Keep the layers wet and cover with a tarp. Stir occasionally to minimize the odor and to move the main decomposition area which will be near the center of the pile.

. . . At the Grocery Store? Pages 158-159

2. The land used for "annual crops" could be put to other uses that would not lead to erosion and the loss of topsoil. The millions of gallons of water used each day to process meat could be saved.
3. Organic foods are grown in soil that relies on crop rotation and recycling organic wastes rather than using fertilizers, insecticides, herbicides and pesticides. The obvious harm of these chemical products includes fouling the waters, the land itself and sometimes affecting the crop being grown.
4. Answers will vary. Possibilities include taking your own grocery bags to the store, which means saving them for reuse; encouraging grocers to stock more organic foods, and to buy more foods in containers that can be reused or recycled.

. . . In My Community? Pages 160-161

1. Answers will vary but could include offering citizens free recycling bins, refusing to pick up trash that isn't sorted and monetary rewards for following the path of recycling.
2. Keep all such containers in a separate place. Make certain lids are still tightly on cans, etc. When they accumulate, contact local public works department for direction on where to take them. Help organize a local campaign to get the entire community to do the same.
3. Answers will vary. Accept any reasonable response.
4. If the meat in the burger came from beef that was raised in an area that was a tropical rain forest only a short time ago, the bird could be further endangered. Some fast-food chains buy cheap beef from Central and South American countries. They should be encouraged to stop.

A Final Note Pages 165-166

1. practice methods that will help to use the cycles of nature naturally, so that ecosystems go on endlessly, boycott fast-food restaurants that buy their beef from countries where rain forests are being slashed and burned, reform is needed in the ownership of rain forests to protect them from destruction
2. greater controls to protect the habitats of wild animals, create more wildlife parks and refuges
3. ban the use of chlorofluorocarbons
4. more organic farming which helps to retain the moisture and keep soil from drying and blowing away, plant trees and grasses to hold the soil
5. better irrigation techniques, plant more trees to hold moisture and soil
6. prevent further destruction of the rain forests, which would allow more trees to use up more carbon dioxide to lessen the effect; use less energy to lessen the greenhouse effect
7. recycle, change in life-style to avoid waste, find substitutes and synthetics that can be used in place of natural resources
8. renewable energy sources, greater reliance on solar power, find alternatives to pesticides and herbicides used in farming, improve filtering systems for cars and factories
9. The sunflower represents regrowth of a more ecologically concerned society.

GA130℠